Additional praise for *Big Data, Data Mining, and Machine Learning: Value Creation for Business Leaders and Practitioners*

"Jared's book is a great introduction to the area of High Powered Analytics. It will be useful for those who have experience in predictive analytics but who need to become more versed in how technology is changing the capabilities of existing methods and creating new possibilities. It will also be helpful for business executives and IT professionals who'll need to make the case for building the environments for, and reaping the benefits of, the next generation of advanced analytics."

—Jonathan Levine, Senior Director, Consumer Insight Analysis at Marriott International

"The ideas that Jared describes are the same ideas that being used by our Kaggle contest winners. This book is a great overview for those who want to learn more and gain a complete understanding of the many facets of data mining, knowledge discovery and extracting value from data."

—Anthony Goldbloom Founder and CEO of Kaggle

"The concepts that Jared presents in this book are extremely valuable for the students that I teach and will help them to more fully understand the power that can be unlocked when an organization begins to take advantage of its data. The examples and case studies are particularly useful for helping students to get a vision for what is possible. Jared's passion for analytics comes through in his writing, and he has done a great job of making complicated ideas approachable to multiple audiences."

—Tonya Etchison Balan, Ph.D., Professor of Practice, Statistics, Poole College of Management, North Carolina State University

Big Data, Data Mining, and Machine Learning

Wiley & SAS Business Series

The Wiley & SAS Business Series presents books that help senior-level managers with their critical management decisions.

Titles in the Wiley & SAS Business Series include:

For more information on any of the above titles, please visit www.wiley.com.

Big Data, Data Mining, and Machine Learning

Value Creation for Business Leaders and Practitioners

Jared Dean

Hai wei,
Great to have you
at the SAS GBC.
Good luck in your analytic
journey.

[signed] Jared Dean

Nov '17

WILEY

Library of Congress Cataloging-in-Publication Data:

Dean, Jared, 1978-
    Big data, data mining, and machine learning : value creation for business leaders and practitioners / Jared Dean.
        1 online resource.—(Wiley & SAS business series)
    Includes index.
    ISBN 978-1-118-92069-5 (ebk); ISBN 978-1-118-92070-1 (ebk);
ISBN 978-1-118-61804-2 (hardback)   1. Management—Data processing.
2. Data mining.   3. Big data.   4. Database management.   5. Information technology—Management.   I. Title.
    HD30.2
    658′.05631—dc23
                                                        2014009116

Printed in the United States of America
10 9 8 7 6 5

To my wife, without whose help, love, and devotion,
this book would not exist. Thank you, Katie!

For Geoffrey, Ava, Mason, and Chase: Remember that the
quickest path to easy is through hard.

Contents

Foreword

I love the field of predictive analytics and have lived in this world for my entire career. The mathematics are fun (at least for me), but turning what the algorithms uncover into solutions that a company uses and generates profit from makes the mathematics worthwhile. In some ways, Jared Dean and I are unusual in this regard; we really do love seeing these solutions work for organizations we work with. What amazes us, though, is that this field that we used to do in the back office, a niche of a niche, has now become one of the sexiest jobs of the twenty-first century. How did this happen?

We live in a world where data is collected in ever-increasing amounts, summarizing more of what people and machines do, and capturing finer granularity of their behavior. These three ways to characterize data are sometimes described as volume, variety, and velocity—the definition of big data. They are collected because of the perceived value in the data even if we don't know exactly what we will do with it. Initially, many organizations collect it and report summaries, often using approaches from business intelligence that have become commonplace.

But in recent years, a paradigm shift has taken place. Organizations have found that predictive analytics transforms the way they make decisions. The algorithms and approaches to predictive modeling described in this book are not new for the most part; Jared himself describes the big-data problem as nothing new. The algorithms he describes are all at least 15 years old, a testimony to their effectiveness that fundamentally new algorithms are not needed. Nevertheless, predictive modeling is in fact new to many organizations as they try to improve decisions with data. These organizations need to gain an understanding not only of the science and principles of predictive modeling but how to apply the principles to problems that defy the standard approaches and answers.

But there is much more to predictive modeling than just building predictive models. The operational aspects of predictive modeling projects are often overlooked and are rarely covered in books and courses. First, this includes specifying hardware and software needed for a predictive modeling. As Jared describes, this depends on the organization, the data, and the analysts working on the project. Without setting up analysts with the proper resources, projects flounder and often fail. I've personally witnessed this on projects I have worked on, where hardware was improperly specified causing me to spend a considerable amount of time working around the limitations in RAM and processing speed.

Ultimately, the success of predictive modeling projects is measured by the metric that matters to the organization using it, whether it be increased efficiency, ROI, customer lifetime value, or soft metrics like company reputation. I love the case studies in this book that address these issues, and you have a half-dozen here to whet your appetite. This is especially important for managers who are trying to understand how predictive modeling will impact their bottom line.

Predictive modeling is science, but successful implementation of predictive modeling solutions requires connecting the models to the business. Experience is essential to recognize these connections, and there is a wealth of experience here to draw from to propel you in your predictive modeling journey.

Dean Abbott
Abbott Analytics, Inc.
March 2014

Preface

This book project was first presented to me during my first week in my current role of managing the data mining development at SAS. Writing a book has always been a bucket-list item, and I was very excited to be involved. I've come to realize why so many people want to write books, but why so few get the chance to see their thoughts and ideas bound and published.

I've had the opportunity during my studies and professional career to be front and center to some great developments in the area of data mining and to study under some brilliant minds. This experience helped position me with the skills and experience I needed to create this work.

Data mining is a field I love. Ever since childhood, I've wanted to explain how things work and understand how systems function both in the "average" case but also at the extremes. From elementary school through high school, I thought engineering would be the job that would couple both my curiosity and my desire to explain the world around me. However, before my last year as an undergraduate student, I found statistics and information systems, and I was hooked.

In Part One of the book, I explore the foundations of hardware and system architecture. This is a love that my parents were kind enough to indulge me in, in a day when computers cost much much more than $299. The first computer in my home was an Apple IIc, with two 5.25" floppy disk drives and no hard drive. A few years later I built an Intel 386 PC from a kit, and I vividly remember playing computer games and hitting the turbo button to move the CPU clock speed from 8 MHz to 16 MHz. I've seen Moore's Law firsthand, and it still amazes me that my smartphone holds more computing power than the computers used in the Mercury space program, the Apollo space program, and the Orbiter space shuttle program combined.

After I finished my undergraduate degree in statistics, I began to work for the federal government at the U.S. Bureau of the Census. This is where I got my first exposure to big data. Prior to joining the Census

Bureau, I had never written a computer program that took more than a minute to run (unless the point was to make the program run for more than a minute). One of my first projects was working with the Master Address File (MAF),[1] which is an address list maintained by the Census Bureau. This address list is also the primary survey frame for current surveys that the Census Bureau administers (yes, there is lots of work to do the other nine years). The list has more than 300 million records, and combining all the address information, longitudinal information, and geographic information, there are hundreds of attributes associated with each housing unit. Working with such a large data set was where I first learned about programming efficiency, scalability, and hardware optimization. I'm grateful to my patient manager, Maryann, who gave me the time to learn and provided me with interesting, valuable projects that gave me practical experience and the opportunity to innovate. It was a great position because I got to try new techniques and approaches that had not been studied before in that department. As with any new project, some ideas worked great and others failed. One specific project I was involved in was trying to identify which blocks (the Census Bureau has the United States divided up into unique geographic areas—the hierarchy is state, county, track, block group, and block; there are about 8.2 million blocks in the United States) from Census 2000 had been overcounted or undercounted. Through the available data, we did not have a way to verify that our model for predicting the deviation of actual housing unit count from reported housing unit count was accurate. The program was fortunate to have funding from congress to conduct field studies to provide feedback and validation of the models. This was the first time I had heard the term "data mining" and I was first exposed to SAS™ Enterprise Miner® and CART® by Salford Systems. After a period of time working for the Census Bureau, I realized that I needed more education to achieve my career goals, and so I enrolled in the statistics department at George Mason University in Fairfax, VA.

During graduate school, I learned in more detail about the algorithms common to the fields of data mining, machine learning, and statistics; these included survival analysis, survey sampling, and

---

[1] The MAF is created during decennial census operations for every housing unit, or potential housing unit, in the United States.

computational statistics. Through my graduate studies, I was able to merge the lessons taught in the classroom to the practical data analysis and innovations required in the office. I acquired an understanding of the theory and the relative strengths and weaknesses of different approaches for data analysis and predictive analytics.

After graduate school, I changed direction in my career, moving from a data analysis[2] role and becoming a software developer. I went to work for SAS Institute Inc., where I was participating in the creation of the software that I had previously used. I had moved from using the software to building it. This presented new challenges and opportunities for growth as I learned about the rigorous numerical validation that SAS imposes on the software, along with its thorough documentation and tireless effort to make new software enhancements consistent with existing software and to consistently deliver new software features that customers need.

During my years at SAS, I've come to thoroughly understand how the software is made and how our customers use it. I often get the chance to visit with customers, listen to their business challenges, and recommend methods or process that help lead them to success; creating value for their organizations.

It is from this collection of experience that I wrote this book, along with the help of the wonderful staff and my colleagues both inside and outside of SAS Institute.

---

[2] I was a data scientist before the term was invented

Acknowledgments

I would like to thank all those who helped me to make this book a reality. It was a long journey and a wonderful learning and growing experience.

Patrick Hall, thank you for your validation of my ideas and contributing many of your own. I appreciate that I could discuss ideas and trends with you and get thoughtful, timely, and useful feedback.

Joseph Pingenot, Ilknur Kabul, Jorge Silva, Larry Lewis, Susan Haller, and Wendy Czika, thank you for sharing your domain knowledge and passion for analytics.

Michael Wallis, thank you for your help in the text analytics area and developing the *Jeopardy!* example.

Udo Sglavo and Taiyeong Lee, thank you for reviewing and offering significant contributions in the analysis of times series data mining.

Barbara Walters and Vicki Jones, thank you for all the conversations about reads and feeds in understanding how the hardware impacted the software.

Jared Peterson for his help in downloading the data from my Nike+ FuelBand.

Franklin So, thank you for your excellent description of a customer's core business problem.

Thank you Grandma Catherine Coyne, who sacrificed many hours to help a fellow author in editing the manuscript to greatly improve its readability. I am very grateful for your help and hope that when I am 80-something I can be half as active as you are.

I would also like to thank the staff of SAS Press and John Wiley & Sons for the feedback and support through all phases of this project, including some major detours along the way.

Finally, I need to acknowledge my wife, Katie, for shouldering many burdens as I researched, wrote, edited, and wrote more. Meeting you was the best thing that has happened to me in my whole life.

Introduction

*Hiding within those mounds of data is knowledge that
could change the life of a patient, or change the world.*

—Atul Butte, Stanford University

"Cancer" is the term given for a class of diseases in which abnormal cells divide in an uncontrolled fashion and invade body tissues. There are more than 100 unique types of cancer. Most are named after the location (usually an organ) where they begin. Cancer begins in the cells of the body. Under normal circumstances, the human body controls the production of new cells to replace cells that are old or have become damaged. Cancer is not normal. In patients with cancer, cells do not die when they are supposed to and new cells form when they are not needed (like when I ask my kids to use the copy machine and I get back ten copies instead of the one I asked for). The extra cells may form a mass of tissue; this is referred to as a tumor. Tumors come in two varieties: benign tumors, which are not cancerous, and malignant tumors, which are cancerous. Malignant tumors spread through the body and invade the tissue. My family, like most I know, has lost a family member to the disease. There were an estimated 1.6 million new cases of cancer in the United States in 2013 and more than 580,000 deaths as a result of the disease.

An estimated 235,000 people in the United States were diagnosed with breast cancer in 2014, and about 40,000 people will die in 2014 as a result of the disease. The most common type of breast cancer is ductal carcinoma, which begins in the lining of the milk ducts. The next most common type of breast cancer is lobular carcinoma. There are a number of treatment options for breast cancer including surgery, chemotherapy, radiation therapy, immunotherapy, and vaccine therapy. Often one or more of the treatment options is used to help ensure the best outcome for patients. About 60 different drugs are approved by the Food and Drug Administration (FDA) for the treatment of breast cancer. The course of treatment and which drug protocols should be used is decided based on consultation between the doctor and patient, and a number of factors go into those decisions.

One of the FDA-approved drug treatments for breast cancer is tamoxifen citrate. It is sold under the brand name of Nolvadex and was first prescribed in 1969 in England but approved by the FDA in 1998. Tamoxifen is normally taken as a daily tablet with doses of 10 mg, 20 mg, or 40 mg. It carries a number of side effects including nausea, indigestion, and leg cramps. Tamoxifen has been used to treat millions of women and men diagnosed with hormone-receptor-positive breast cancer. Tamoxifen is often one of the first drugs prescribed for treating breast cancer because it has a high success rate of around 80%.

Learning that a drug is 80% successful gives us hope that tamoxifen will provide good patient outcomes, but there is one important detail about the drug that was not known until the big data era. It is that tamoxifen is not 80% effective in patients but 100% effective in 80% of patients and ineffective in the rest. That is a life-changing finding for thousands of people each year. Using techniques and ideas discussed in this book, scientists were able to identify genetic markers that can identify, in advance, if tamoxifen will effectively treat a person diagnosed with breast cancer. This type of analysis was not possible before the era of big data. Why was it not possible? Because the volume and granularity of the data was missing; volume came from pooling patient results and granularity came from DNA sequencing. In addition to the data, the computational resources needed to solve a problem like this were not readily available to most scientists outside of the super computing lab. Finally the third component, the algorithms or modeling techniques needed to understand this relationship, have matured greatly in recent years.

The story of Tamoxifen highlights the exciting opportunities that are available to us as we have more and more data along with computing resources and algorithms that aid in classification and prediction. With knowledge like that was gained by the scientists studying tamoxifen, we can begin to reshape the treatment of disease and disrupt positively many other areas of our lives. With these advances we can avoid giving the average treatment to everyone but instead determine which people will be helped by a particular drug. No longer will a drug be 5% effective; now we can identify which 5% of patients the drug will help. The concept of personalized medicine has been discussed for many years. With advances in working with big data and improved predictive analytics, it is more of a reality than ever. A drug with a 2% success rate will never be pursued by a drug manufacturer or approved by the FDA unless it can be determined which patients it will help. If that information exists, then lives can be saved. Tamoxifen is one of many examples that show us the potential that exists if we can take advantage of the computational resources and are patient enough to find value in the data that surrounds us.

We are currently living in the big data era. That term "big data" was first coined around the time the big data era began. While I consider the big data era to have begun in 2001, the date is the source of some debate and impassioned discussion on blogs—and even the *New York Times*. The term "big data" appears to have been first used, with its currently understood context, in the late 1990s. The first academic paper was presented in 2000, and published in 2003, by Francis X. Diebolt— "Big Data Dynamic Factor Models for Macroeconomic Measurement and Forecasting"—but credit is largely given to John Mashey, the chief scientist for SGI, as the first person to use the term "big data." In the late 1990s, Mashey gave a series of talks to small groups about this big data tidal wave that was coming. The big data era is an era described by rapidly expanding data volumes, far beyond what most people imagined would ever occur.

The large data volume does not solely classify this as the big data era, because there have always been data volumes larger than our ability to effectively work with the data have existed. What sets the current time apart as the big data era is that companies, governments, and nonprofit organizations have experienced a shift in behavior. In this era, they want to start using all the data that it is possible for them to collect, for a current or future unknown purpose, to improve their business. It is widely believed, along with significant support through research and case studies, that organizations that use data to make decisions over time in fact do make better decisions, which leads to a stronger, more viable business. With the velocity at which data is created increasing at such a rapid rate, companies have responded by keeping every piece of data they could possibly capture and valuing the future potential of that data higher than they had in the past. How much personal data do we generate? The first question is: What is personal data? In 1995, the European Union in privacy legislation defined it as any information that could identify a person, directly or indirectly. International Data Corporation (IDC) estimated that 2.8 zettabytes[1] of data were created in 2012 and that the amount of data generated each year will double by 2015. With such a large figure, it is hard to understand how much of that data is actually about you. It breaks down to about 5 gigabytes of data per day for the average American office worker. This data consists of email, downloaded movies, streamed audio, Excel spreadsheets, and so on. In this data also includes the data that is generated as information moves throughout the Internet. Much of this generated data is not seen directly by you or me but is stored about us. Some examples of nondirect data are things like traffic camera footage, GPS coordinates from our phones, or toll transactions as we speed through automated E-ZPass lanes.

Before the big data era began, businesses assigned relatively low value to the data they were collecting that did not have immediate value. When the big data era began, this investment in collecting and storing data for its potential future value changed, and organizations made a conscious effort to keep every potential bit of data. This shift in behavior created a virtuous circle where data was stored and then, because data was available, people were assigned to find value in it for the organization. The success in finding value led to more data being gathered and so on. Some of the data stored was a dead end, but many times the

---

[1] A zettabyte is 1 billion terabytes.

results were confirmed that the more data you have, the better off you are likely to be. The other major change in the beginning of the big data era was the rapid development, creation, and maturity of technologies to store, manipulate, and analyze this data in new and efficient ways.

Now that we are in the big data era, our challenge is not getting data but getting the right data and using computers to augment our domain knowledge and identify patterns that we did not see or could not find previously.

Some key technologies and market disruptions have led us to this point in time where the amount of data being collected, stored, and considered in analytical activities has grown at a tremendous rate. This is due to many factors including Internet Protocol version 6 (IPv6), improved telecommunications equipment, technologies like RFID, telematics sensors, the reduced per unit cost of manufacturing electronics, social media, and the Internet.

Here is a timeline that highlights some of the key events leading up to the big data era and events that continue to shape the usage of big data and the future of analytics.

BIG DATA TIMELINE

Here are a number of items that show influential events that prepared the way for the big data era and significant milestones during the era.

1991

- The Internet, or World Wide Web as we know it, is born. The protocol Hypertext Transfer Protocol (HTTP) becomes the standard means for sharing information in this new medium.

1995

- Sun releases the Java platform. Java, invented in 1991, has become the second most popular language behind C. It dominates the Web applications space and is the de facto standard for middle-tier applications. These applications are the source for recording and storing web traffic.
- Global Positioning System (GPS) becomes fully operational. GPS was originally developed by DARPA (Defense Advanced Research Projects Agency) for military applications in the early 1970s.

This technology has become omnipresent in applications for car and airline navigation and finding a missing iPhone.

1998

- Carlo Strozzi develops an open-source relational database and calls it NoSQL. Ten years later, a movement to develop NoSQL databases to work with large, unstructured data sets gains momentum.

- Google is founded by Larry Page and Sergey Brin, who worked for about a year on a Stanford search engine project called BackRub.

1999

- Kevin Ashton, cofounder of the Auto-ID Center at the Massachusetts Institute of Technology (MIT), invents the term "the Internet of Things."

2001

- Wikipedia is launched. The crowd-sourced encyclopedia revolutionized the way people reference information.

2002

- Version 1.1 of the Bluetooth specification is released by the Institute of Electrical and Electronics Engineers (IEEE). Bluetooth is a wireless technology standard for the transfer of data over short distances. The advancement of this specification and its adoption lead to a whole host of wearable devices that communicate between the device and another computer. Today nearly every portable device has a Bluetooth receiver.

2003

- According to studies by IDC and EMC, the amount of data created in 2003 surpasses the amount of data created in all of human history before then. It is estimated that 1.8 zettabytes (ZB) was created in 2011 alone (1.8 ZB is the equivalent of 200 billion high-definition movies, each two hours long, or 47 million years of footage with no bathroom breaks).

- LinkedIn, the popular social networking website for professionals, launches. In 2013, the site had about 260 million users.

2004

■ Wikipedia reaches 500,000 articles in February; seven months later it tops 1 million articles.

■ Facebook, the social networking service, is founded by Mark Zuckerberg and others in Cambridge, Massachusetts. In 2013, the site had more than 1.15 billion users.

2005

■ The Apache Hadoop project is created by Doug Cutting and Mike Caferella. The name for the project came from the toy elephant of Cutting's young son. The now-famous yellow elephant becomes a household word just a few years later and a foundational part of almost all big data strategies.

■ The National Science Board recommends that the National Science Foundation (NSF) create a career path for "a sufficient number of high-quality data scientists" to manage the growing collection of digital information.

2007

■ Apple releases the iPhone and creates a strong consumer market for smartphones.

2008

■ The number of devices connected to the Internet exceeds the world's population.

2011

■ IBM's Watson computer scans and analyzes 4 terabytes (200 million pages) of data in seconds to defeat two human players on the television show *Jeopardy!* (There is more about the show in Part Two.)

■ Work begins in UnQL, a query language for NoSQL databases.

■ The available pools in the IPv4 address space have all been assigned. IPv4 is a standard for assigning an Internet protocol (IP) address. The IPv4 protocol was based on a 32-bit number, meaning there are 2^{32} or 4.5 billion unique addresses available. This event shows the real demand and quantity of Internet-connected devices.

2012

- The Obama administration announces the Big Data Research and Development Initiative, consisting of 84 programs in six departments. The NSF publishes "Core Techniques and Technologies for Advancing Big Data Science & Engineering."

- IDC and EMC estimate that 2.8 ZB of data will be created in 2012 but that only 3% of what could be usable for big data is tagged and less is analyzed. The report predicts that the digital world will by 2020 hold 40 ZB, 57 times the number of grains of sand on all the beaches in the world.

- The *Harvard Business Review* calls the job of data scientist "the sexiest job of the 21st century."

2013

- The democratization of data begins. With smartphones, tablets, and Wi-Fi, everyone generates data at prodigious rates. More individuals access large volumes of public data and put data to creative use.

The events of the last 20 years have fundamentally changed the way data is treated. We create more of it each day; it is not a waste product but a buried treasure waiting to be discovered by curious, motivated researchers and practitioners who see these trends and are reaching out to meet the current challenges.

WHY THIS TOPIC IS RELEVANT NOW

You've read this far in the book because I expect you are looking for ideas and information to help you turn data into information and knowledge. What I hope you learn in the subsequent pages are strategies and concrete ideas for accomplishing your business objective or personal edification regarding how you can harness the data to better your situation, whether in the office, the home, or a fantasy football league.

You should also understand that this is not a new problem—data has always been "too big" to work with effectively. This problem has only been exacerbated as now individuals are generating so much more data than ever before as they go through their daily lives. This increase in data, however, has caused the information management industry to provide better solutions than ever on how to store, manage, and analyze the data we are producing.

In addition, we also have more opportunity to engage with data. A simple example that is discussed in more detail in Part Two is the recommendations you get from Amazon. That small application at the bottom of its web pages illustrates this point very well. In order to make these recommendations, Amazon can use a few different techniques that mostly center on three pieces of information; how you are similar to other shoppers, similar shoppers' opinions of the product you are viewing, and what product similar shoppers ultimately purchased. Alternatively, Amazon could make recommendations from an item point of view. Take, for example, my recent purchase of a baseball glove. The recommendations included items like baseball bats, baseballs, baseball glove oil, and other baseball-related equipment. These recommendations are based on item-to-item recommendations. Baseball gloves are usually sold with baseballs, bats, and glove oil so Amazon recommends them to me. The other method is to look at my profile and find users who have purchased similar items or have similar details as they relate to Amazon and then recommend to me what they purchased. To be effective at making recommendations requires a real commitment to recording, storing, and analyzing extremely large volumes of data.

I think you only need to look up from this book to see a device that is generating data at this very moment. That data will soon be used to inform some business process, recommendation, or public safety issue. This not a future or theoretical problem, this is now.

IS BIG DATA A FAD?

> *Data! Data! Data! he cried impatiently. I can't make bricks without clay!*
>
> —Sherlock Holmes, "The Adventure in the Copper Beeches"

Many informed individuals in the analytics and information technology (IT) communities are becoming sensitive to the actual term "big data." It has no doubt been co-opted for self-promotion by many people and organizations with little or no ties to storing and processing large amounts of data or data that requires large amounts of computation. Aside from marketing and promotional mischaracterizations, the term has become vague to the point of near meaninglessness even in some technical situations. "Big data" once meant petabyte scale, unstructured chunks of data mined or generated from the Internet.

I submit that "big data" has expanded to mean a situation where the logistics of storing, processing, or analyzing data have surpassed traditional operational abilities of organizations; said another way, you now have too much data to store effectively or compute efficiently using traditional methods. This may also include having too little time to process the data to use the information to make decisions. In addition, big data means using all available data in your models, not just samples. Big data indicates the capability of using entire data sets instead of just segments as in years past. In the purview of wider popular usage, the definition of this term will likely continue to broaden.

For certain leaders in the field, "big data" is fast becoming, or perhaps always was, just data. These people are long accustomed to dealing with the large amounts of data that other fields are just beginning to mine for information. For evidence, look to the larger web companies and certain entities within the U.S. government that have been using extremely large amounts of unstructured data operationally for years, long before anyone ever coined the term "big data." To them, it was just "data." In addition, the big banks and insurance companies have been pushing up against the limits of commercial, column-oriented data storage technologies for decades, and to them this was just "data" too. Consider whether the scale at which Google is indexing all available information, or which the National Security Agency is recording, has really changed since before the term "big data" entered the popular lexicon. It was difficult to comprehend how much data this was before, and it is still is just as hard to comprehend. However, to these leaders in the field, dealing with it is just a day's work. The rest of world is now joining these industries in storing, computing, and analyzing these immense amounts of data, and now we have a word to describe it and a time period to reference. Figure I.1 shows the popularity of the term "big data" as it came into common usage beginning in 2011. Since the 1940s when computer was a job title or in the 1960s when file transfer involved

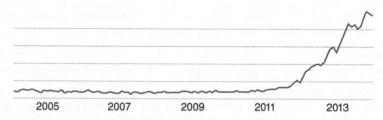

Figure I.1 Trend of Google Searches of "Big Data" over Time Showing the Popularity of the Term
Source: Google Trends

moving a carton of punch cards from one location to another and hoping you did not trip, organizations have had data challenges. Today those challenges are just on a larger scale. Nearly every company must deal with these challenges or accept the idea that the company itself may become irrelevant. *Forbes* in 2013 published an article that said that companies without a big data strategy miss out on $71.2 million per year. If you could raise revenue over $70 million this year and each subsequent year, I am sure your future would be very bright in your organization. The key to capitalize on this opportunity is to have a well-thought-out strategy on big data and execute to the strategy.

To be clear, the solutions surrounding the storage, processing, and analyzing "big data" are not a fad even if the term turns out to be one. Although some are overhyped right now, they are extremely valuable and in some cases actually revolutionary technologies. They have drawn such attention for this reason. Data is not magic—it's just a valuable raw material that can be refined and distilled into valuable specific insights. These insights are then converted to information that eventually creates knowledge.

The bigger the data, the more resource-intensive it is to work with, the better the value of the information must be to make the trade-off a wise business decision. While there is simply no underlying principle stating that the size of data is positively correlated with its value, the size of a data set is positively correlated with its cost to maintain. The value of using big data is defined by how valuable the information gleaned from its process is compared to the time and resources it took to process that information.

This being said, there is a great deal of evidence that prudent data analysis can create value, whether knowledge or monetary, for most organizations. This is why the technologies that allow us to store, process, and analyze large amounts of data will continue to receive increased usage and are anything but a passing fad. For the leading analytic companies and entities, using large amounts of data has been a favorable value proposition for some time, and there is no reason for that trend to decelerate.

Data is the new oil. It has all of the same challenges in that it is plentiful but difficult and sometimes messy to extract. There are a few entities that control most of it, and a vast infrastructure has been built to transport, refine, and distribute it. With the performance of the required technologies increasing and their prices decreasing, if organizations currently struggle to deal efficiently with the medium-size data, they will be ill prepared and at a strategic disadvantage against their competition when data sizes increase, which they inevitably will do. If nothing else, companies, hospitals, and universities will face competition that will drive them to adopt technology to handle the growing volume of data. Other organizations, such as nongovernmental agencies, may be slower to invest in the new generation of data technologies and personnel. This is due to planning and implementation costs as well as the shortage of analytical professionals needed to produce value from this significant investment in hardware human capital; and some smaller organizations will not need sophisticated analysis to understand their operational environment.

WHERE USING BIG DATA MAKES A BIG DIFFERENCE

There have been so many news stories and hype about big data, and how it can transform your business, that it begins to sound like something you would find in Shangri-La. It is often portrayed as the answer to all things that cause problems for organizations. There are promises that it will identify the right customers for marketing campaigns and help academic institutions select the perfect students for their admissions process. Don't let skepticism turn you into a cynic.

It is indeed true that having more data, especially historical data, often will help model predictions be more accurate. Using additional sources of data, such as social networks, will help organizations make better predictions about customer choices and preferences, because all of us are influenced to some degree by those in our social network, either the physical or the virtual one.

Consider a situation where I have a poor customer experience with my cable provider; so poor that I cancel all of my services and look for another provider. Does this situation make my friends, family, and associates more likely or less likely purchase new services? How does that knowledge of my cancellation because of poor customer service, along with knowing my close friends, family, and associates, affect the cable provider's action? This is a prime example of big data in action; five to ten years ago, this type of analysis would not have been possible because the data sources just did not exist. The answer to my question of how this affects those who know is that my family and friends are less likely to add new services and potentially may follow suit and cancel their cable service as well. Having more data about your customers, products, and processes allows you to consider these types of effects in predicting customers' future behavior. It also needs to be pointed out that having the data and doing the analysis are vital steps to taking advantage of the opportunity in the big data era, but unless the organization is equipped to use new data sources and methods in their processes and act on this information, all of the data and the best analysis in the world will not help it improve.

There is danger in not taking the time to know how much weight to give to this large amount of newly available information, when that information is compared to all of the other attributes that affect a person's decision-making process. Returning to the poor customer service and my social network example, it is clear that the people in my social network are now more likely to cancel services, but how much more likely? One company that takes many different metrics and creates a single aggregate score is Klout; the higher your Klout score, the more influential you are online. Klout uses comments, mentions, retweets, likes and so on to create this score. The company is able to measure online influence only because that is all the data to which it has access.

The question of sampling and big data is a hotly debated topic, and I have read and heard on several occasions that sampling is dead. As a trained statistician and former employee of the U.S. Census Bureau, I would never say that sampling is dead or that it has no place in business today. Sampling is useful and valid. For certain types of problems, sampling from the population yields just as good a result as performing the same analysis using the entire population (all the data).

However, sampling cannot meet the objectives of many critical high-value projects, such as finding outliers. Companies that cling to sampling will miss out on opportunities to learn insights that can be found only by considering all the data. Outliers are one such example. In a statistical case, the term "outliers" usually has a negative connotation. But in many business problems, the outliers are your most profitable customers or the new market segments that can be exploited.

The best advice is to be an informed data user. Having seven years of customer history instead of three in August 2008 would not have helped in any way to predict people's upcoming spending habits in the United States. In just a few weeks, the financial markets were going to collapse and several large investment firms were going to declare bankruptcy or be purchased at fire sale prices. The U.S. government would begin a massive bailout of the financial markets that would, in some way, affect everyone in the industrialized world. No amount of data would have helped. No amount of data analysis modeling of the preceding months' spending could forecast what the months after the bailout would look like for the average consumer. In order to build useful models in that time, you needed competent practitioners who understood how to simulate and adjust for economic conditions that no one in the workforce had seen before.

There are, however, two major advantages of using all the available data in solving your analytical business problems. The first is technical, and the other is productivity through an improved workflow for analysts.

Technical Issue

Many statistical and machine learning techniques are averaging processes. An averaging process is an algorithm or methodology that seeks to minimize or maximize the overall error and therefore make the best prediction for the average situation. Two examples of averaging algorithms are linear regression and neural networks. Both of these methods are explained in more detail in Part Two, but for now understand that regression seeks to minimize the overall error by fitting a line that minimizes the squared distance from the line to the data points. The square is used because the distances from the line to the data points will be both negative and positive. A neural network works by connecting all the input, or dependent variables, to a hidden set of variables and iteratively reweighting the connections between them until the classification of the holdout sample cannot be improved.

These averaging methods can be used on big data, and they will work very well. It is also very common for these methods to be very efficient in processing the data due to clever and persistent developers who have organized the computation in a way that takes advantage of modern computing systems. These systems, which have multiple cores, can each be working on a part of the problem; to get even greater speedups, multiple computers can be used in a distributed computing environment. Nonparametric techniques, such as a rank sign test, also fall into this category of an averaging model technique. I call this type of algorithm an averaging model process. Because we are seeking to average, sampling is a potential substitute that can provide comparable answers.

However, a second class of modeling problem is not averaging but is an extremity-based model or tail-based modeling process. These model types are used for a different objective and seek to find extreme or unusual values. These are sometimes referred to as outliers, but not in the strict statistical scenes. Instead, there are notable and unusual points or segments that are often the problems that are the most challenging to companies and carry the biggest return on investment in the present business climate. Examples of tail-based processes are fraud detection, offer optimization, manufacturing quality control, or microsegmentation in marketing.

Next I show why it is imperative to use complete data sets in these types of problems from several different industries and domains. In these cases and many others, these problems cannot be solved effectively without all the data, which is large and complex.

Fraud

If the rate of credit card fraud is 1 in 1,000 transactions,[2] and you sample 20% of your data to build your fraud model, it is likely that you will not have a single fraudulent activity. In fact, if you take anything less than all the data, you likely will never include the fraudulent activity. Predictive models work by using past performance to identify current behavior that has the same characteristics. Without having those fraudulent transactions, you will lack enough information to create an equation that can recognize fraud when it is happening. It is necessary to capture and analyze past fraudulent activity to create effective models for predicting future fraudulent activity.

In addition, if you are sampling the current incoming credit card transactions looking for fraud, you will miss those transactions that could have been flagged had they been present in the data being analyzed.

Optimization

For the optimization family of problems, consider the example of U.S. commercial airline traffic. If we want to understand the congestion points in the air traffic network, or model the effect of a tornado in Dallas, or a tropical storm in Miami, we need to use the entire data set. This is necessary to measure and accurately describe the scope of the problem and its effects on overall flight delays or cancellations and measure the costs to the industry. Imagine if a sample was taken in this case. First we would have to design a sampling scheme. Do you take a sequential sample of every tenth flight across the system? Do you weigh each airport by the number of commercial flights that occur there on the average day? Do you use a random sample? All of these schemes have shortfalls in seeing the complete picture, and those shortfalls will be most prominent in the calculation of the standard error and the confidence intervals of the prediction. To do these calculations correctly will take time to measure, calculate, and verify. If it is not done correctly, then your answer is wrong, but you will never know. The sampling also requires a front-loaded investment; before

---

[2] The incidence rate is actually much smaller, but this makes for easier math.

I can work with the sampled data, I have to invest the time to create the sample and validate that it is accurate. I also cannot see any type of result until a significant amount of work is already completed.

Relationship Management

Retention of telecommunications customers is a key component to revenue stream. Consider the challenge of predicting which customers are likely to cancel their contract and move to a different carrier. (This is referred to as attrition or churn.) It would be useful to know the typical behavior patterns of customers in the period of time before they cancel, including whom they call or from whom they receive calls. If you use only 10% of the calls each customer sends or receives, use only 10% of the customers, or look at only 10% of the numbers they call, you could be misled in predicting the true likelihood that a particular customer will cancel their contract. This is true for two reasons; first, since only a small percentage of customers leave each month, it would be probable that not a single dissatisfied costumer (or even a whole segment of customers) would be included in the sample. It would also be possible that some of a dissatisfied customer's calls are not included in the sample. However, without the complete set of calls for a given customer, it is much more difficult to identify the pattern that you are looking for. (This is like working on a puzzle that is missing most of the pieces.) With the inability to identify those customers likely to cancel their contract, the problem will grow over time. Given the significant costs to acquire new customers in the telecommunications market, implementing an effective strategy to keep existing customers is worth millions and millions of dollars in annual revenue.

Work Flow Productivity

The second consideration is ensuring that the productivity of the analyst stays as high as possible. Analytics has become a very hot topic in the past few years, and predictions from McKinsey & Company project a shortfall of 140,000 to 190,000 people with the analytical expertise and 1.5 million managers needed to evaluate and make decisions based on big data. This translates to a deficit of 50% to 60% of the required personnel by the year 2018 in the United States alone.

With this significant shortfall in capable people, the human capital you have already made in your organization needs to be preserved and improved. The analytical talent you already have in your organization will become more scarce as other organizations work to make better use of their big data through better analytics and governance. It will be critical to keep analytical talent engaged and productive.

From the same report:

> "Several issues will have to be addressed to capture the full potential of big data. Policies related to privacy, security, intellectual property, and even liability will need to be addressed in a big data world. Organizations need not only to put the right talent and technology in place but also structure workflows and incentives to optimize the use of big data. Access to data is critical—companies will increasingly need to integrate information from multiple data sources, often from third parties, and the incentives have to be in place to enable this." (McKinsey) www
> .mckinsey.com/insights/business_technology/big_data_the_
> next_frontier_for_innovation

As I mentioned in the prior section, the work to sample is a very front-loaded task; the majority of the work is done before any results can be created or exploration can begin. This is really backward from the optimum work flow. The best thing is to make the access to data exploration and quick modeling against the data simple and readily available. Organizations should enable the "failing fast" paradigm. Fail has a negative connotation, but failing fast is a useful strategy for determining which projects have merit and which do not. When people have the ability to work with the entire set of data, they can explore and prototype in a more efficient and natural way that does not require a great deal of up-front work to access the data. To enable this type of environment for your organization, ongoing commitments to capital and technological investments are required.

Making effective work flow and data computing resources for employees translates to large productivity gains and short timelines to pay back the return on investment. I have seen this transformation first-hand when I was working on a credit card modeling project for a large U.S. bank. Using the traditional methods (hardware and software), it was taking many hours to solve the problem. When I switched to a new distributed computing environment, I was able to solve the same problem in two to three minutes. I no longer had to multitask across so many projects because each one had significant downtime while models were being built. I was able to try a number of algorithms and tune each one to a degree that would not have been possible before. The work flow was reminiscent of class projects in school where data volumes were small and software ran nearly instantaneously. This was the method I had been trained in, and it felt more natural. I saw immediate benefits in the form of better model lift, which the customer saw as millions of dollars in revenue increases.

The Complexities When Data Gets Large

Big data is not inherently harder to analyze than small data. The computation of a mean is still just the sum of the values divided by the number of observations, and computing a frequency table still requires reading the data and storing the number of times a distinct value occurs in the data. Both of these situations can be done by reading the data only one time. However, when data volumes gets large or when the data complexity increases, analytics run times can grow to the point that they take longer to compute than the operational constraints will allow. This can result in misleading results or a failure to find a result at all.

Nonlinear Relationships

In real data, there are often nonlinear relationships between variables. Sometimes these relationships can be described "well enough" using linear relationships, but sometimes they cannot. A linear relationship is sometimes hard to imagine, so let us use exiting a parking lot as an example. My family and a few others attended a symphony performance and fireworks show for the Fourth of July (Independence Day in the United States). We parked near each other in the same section of the parking lot, which was about a seven-minute walk from the venue. After the fireworks concluded, our group made our way to the exit, but one of the families became separated. Instead of taking the closest exit to our seats that is open only after the event, they took a longer route through the venue to the main entrance where we had entered. This alternate route added about three minutes to their departure time. A parking lot after a major event is always something I, as a quantitative person, dread. I easily grow frustrated over inefficiency, and this exit situation is known to be poor and bordering on terrible. My family arrived at the car, loaded our cooler, chairs, and blankets, and began to drive to the exit. Traffic inside the parking lot was quite slow, because of poor visibility and all the pedestrian traffic leaving the venue. We proceeded to move with the traffic and following police direction made it home in about 40 minutes.[3] As we were arriving home, my wife received a text message from our friends who had taken the other exit, asking if we were stuck in the parking lot like they were. So, while our drive took twice as long as it does on a normal day, those three extra minutes added not three minutes (which is what we would expect from a linear relationship between time of departure and time of arrival) to their drive but almost another 45 minutes to their drive home (in addition to the 40 minutes it took my family) from the event. This example is one many can relate to, and it illustrates an important point: Knowing about your data can be a huge asset in applying analytics to your data.

A second example of nonlinear relationship is that of the space shuttle Challenger disaster in 1986. Even though it has been almost 30 years, I still remember sitting in Mrs. Goodman's class in my elementary school, with eager anticipation as we were going to see the Challenger liftoff and take a teacher, Sharon McAuliffe, into space. Many of you know the tragic events of that day and the findings of the NASA Commission. To review the details, 73 seconds after liftoff, the primary and secondary O-rings on the solid-state boosters failed and caused an explosion due to excess hydrogen gas and premature fuel ignition. This resulted in the Challenger being torn apart. The reason the O-rings failed is blamed primarily on the weather. That January day was only about 30 degrees at launch time,[4] much colder than any space shuttle launch NASA had attempted before. The cold weather

---

[3] The drive between my home and the venue takes about 20 minutes on the average day.

[4] The launch control parameters for the Space Shuttle were a 24-hour average temperature of 41 degrees F and not warmer than 99 degrees F for 30 consecutive minutes.

created a problem, because NASA personnel planned assuming a linear relationship between the air temperature and O-ring performance, but instead that relationship was nonlinear and the O-ring was actually much more brittle and ineffective than preplanning had anticipated. This was a tragic lesson to learn as it cost the lives of many remarkable people. After this incident, NASA changed a number of procedures in an effort to make space flight safer.[5]

In statistics, there are several terms of art to describe the shape or distribution of your data. The terms are: mean, standard deviation, skewness, and kurtosis. At this point, the important facts to understand and keep in mind are that: (1) there are often nonlinear relationships in real-world data; (2) as the data size increases, you are able to see those relationships more clearly; and, more frequently (3) nonlinear relationships can have a very significant effect on your results if you do not understand and control for them.

In Part One of this book, the focus is on the technology aspects of creating an analytical environment for data mining, machine learning, and working with big data and the trade-offs that result from certain technology choices. In Part Two, the focus is on algorithms and methods that can be used to gain information from your data. In Part Three, case studies show how, by utilizing these new technology advances and algorithms, organizations were able to make big impacts. Part Three also illustrates that using high-performance computing, analytical staff productivity went up in meaningful ways.

---

[5] I got to witness the safety protocol in action. I was at Cape Canaveral for the launch of STS-111, but it was scrubbed with less than an hour before liftoff.

The Computing Environment

With data collection, "the sooner the better" is always the best answer.

— Marissa Mayer

D ata mining is going through a significant shift with the volume, variety, value and velocity of data increasing significantly each year. The volume of data created is outpacing the amount of currently usable data to such a degree that most organizations do not know what value is in their data. At the same that time data mining is changing, hardware capabilities have also undergone dramatic changes. Just as data mining is not one thing but a collection of many steps, theories, and algorithms, hardware can be dissected into a number of components. The corresponding component changes are not always in sync with this increased demand in data mining, machine learning, and big analytical problems.

The four components of disk, memory, central processing unit, and network can be thought of as four legs of the hardware platform stool. To have a useful stool, all the legs must be of the same length or users will be frustrated, stand up, and walk away to find a better stool; so too must the hardware system for data mining be in balance in regard to the components to give users the best experience for their analytical problems.

Data mining on any scale cannot be done without specialized software. In order to explain the evolution and progression of the hardware, there needs to be a small amount of background on the traditional interaction between hardware and software. Data mining software packages are discussed in detail in Part One.

In the past, traditional data mining software was implemented by loading data into memory and running a single thread of execution over the data. The process was constrained by the amount of memory available and the speed of a processor. If the process could not fit entirely into memory, the process would fail. The single thread of execution also failed to take advantage of multicore servers unless multiple users were on the system at the same time.

The main reason we are seeing dramatic changes in data mining is related to the changes in storage technologies as well as computational capabilities. However, all software packages cannot take advantage of current hardware capacity. This is especially true of the distributed computing model. A careful evaluation should be made to ensure that algorithms are distributed and effectively leveraging all the computing power available to you.

CHAPTER **1**

Hardware

am often asked what the best hardware configuration is for doing
data mining. The only appropriate answer for this type of question is
that it depends on what you are trying to do. There are a number of
considerations to be weighed when deciding how to build an appropriate computing environment for your big data analytics.

STORAGE (DISK)

Storage of data is usually the first thing that comes to mind when the
topic of big data is mentioned. It is the storage of data that allows us to
keep a record of history so that it can be used to tell us what will likely
happen in the future.

A traditional hard drive is made up of platters which are actual
disks coated in a magnetized film that allow the encoding of 1s and 0s
that make up data. The spindles that turn the vertically stacked platters
are a critical part of rating hard drives because the spindles determine
how fast the platters can spin and thus how fast the data can be read
and written. Each platter has a single drive head; they both move in
unison so that only one drive head is reading from a particular platter.

This mechanical operation is very precise and also very slow compared to the other components of the computer. It can be a large

27

contributor to the time required to solve high-performance data mining problems.

To combat the weakness of disk speeds, disk arrays[1] became widely available, and they provide higher throughput. The maximum throughput of a disk array to a single system from external storage subsystems is in the range of 1 to 6 gigabytes (GB) per second (a speedup of 10 to 50 times in data access rates).

Another change in disk drives as a response to the big data era is that their capacity has increased 50% to 100% per year in the last 10 years. In addition, prices for disk arrays have remained nearly constant, which means the price per terabyte (TB) has decreased by half per year.

This increase in disk drive capacity has not been matched by the ability to transfer data to/from the disk drive, which has increased by only 15% to 20% per year. To illustrate this, in 2008, the typical server drive was 500 GB and had a data transfer rate of 98 megabytes per second (MB/sec). The entire disk could be transferred in about 85 minutes (500 GB = 500,000 MB/98 MB/sec). In 2013, there were 4 TB disks that have a transfer rate of 150 MB/sec, but it would take about 440 minutes to transfer the entire disk. When this is considered in light of the amount of data doubling every few years, the problem is obvious. Faster disks are needed.

Solid state devices (SSDs) are disk drives without a disk or any moving parts. They can be thought of as stable memory, and their data read rates can easily exceed 450 MB/sec. For moderate-size data mining environments, SSDs and their superior throughput rates can dramatically change the time to solution. SSD arrays are also available, but SSDs still cost significantly more per unit of capacity than hard disk drives (HDDs). SSD arrays are limited by the same external storage bandwidth as HDD arrays. So although SSDs can solve the data mining problem by reducing the overall time to read and write the data, converting all storage to SSD might be cost prohibitive. In this case, hybrid strategies that use different types of devices are needed.

Another consideration is the size of disk drives that are purchased for analytical workloads. Smaller disks have faster access times, and

---

[1] A disk array is a specialized hardware storage that provides larger storage capacity and data access because of its specialized implementation. NetApp and EMC are two major vendors of disk arrays.

there can be advantages in the parallel disk access that comes from multiple disks reading data at the same time for the same problem. This is an advantage only if the software can take advantage of this type of disk drive configuration.

Historically, only some analytical software was capable of using additional storage to augment memory by writing intermediate results to disk storage. This extended the size of problem that could be solved but caused run times to go up. Run times rose not just because of the additional data load but also due to the slower access of reading intermediate results from disk instead of reading them from memory. For a typical desktop or small server system, data access to storage devices, particularly writing to storage devices, is painfully slow. A single thread of execution for an analytic process can easily consume 100 MB/sec, and the dominant type of data access is sequential read or write. A typical high-end workstation has a15K RPM SAS drive; the drive spins at 15,000 revolutions per minute and uses the SAS technology to read and write data at a rate of 100 to 150 MB/sec. This means that one or two cores can consume all of the disk bandwidth available. It also means that on a modern system with many cores, a large percentage of the central processing unit (CPU) resources will be idle for many data mining activities; this is not a lack of needed computation resources but the mismatch that exists among disk, memory, and CPU.

CENTRAL PROCESSING UNIT

The term "CPU" has had two meanings in computer hardware. CPU is used to refer to the plastic and steel case that holds all the essential elements of a computer. This includes the power supply, motherboard, peripheral cards, and so on. The other meaning of CPU is the processing chip located inside the plastic and steel box. In this book, CPU refers to the chip.

The speed of the CPU saw dramatic improvements in the 1980s and 1990s. CPU speed was increasing at such a rate that single threaded software applications would run almost twice as fast on new CPU versions as they became available. The CPU speedup was described by Gordon Moore, cofounder of Intel, in the famous Moore's law, which is an observation that the number of transistors and integrated circuits that are able to be put in a given area doubles every two years and therefore instructions can be executed at twice the speed. This trend in doubling CPU speed continued into the 1990s, when Intel engineers observed that if the doubling trend continued, the heat that would be emitted from these chips would be as hot as the sun by 2010. In the early 2000s, the Moore's law free lunch was over, at least in terms of processing speed. Processor speeds (frequencies) stalled, and computer companies sought new ways to increase performance. Vector units, present in limited form in x86 since the Pentium MMX instructions, were increasingly important to attaining performance and gained additional features, such as single- and then double-precision floating point.

In the early 2000s, then, chip manufacturers also turned to adding extra threads of execution into their chips. These multicore chips were scaled-down versions of the multiprocessor supercomputers, with the cores sharing resources such as cache memory. The number of cores located on a single chip has increased over time; today many server machines offer two six-core CPUs.

In comparison to hard disk data access, CPU access to memory is faster than a speeding bullet; the typical access is in the range of 10 to 30 GB/sec. All other components of the computer are racing to keep up with the CPU.

Graphical Processing Unit

The graphical processing unit (GPU) has gotten considerable publicity as an unused computing resource that could reduce the run times of data mining and other analytical problems by parallelizing the computations. The GPU is already found in every desktop computer in the world.

In the early 2000s, GPUs got into the computing game. Graphics processing has evolved considerably from early text-only displays of the first desktop computers. This quest for better graphics has been driven by industry needs for visualization tools. One example is engineers using three-dimensional (3D) computer-aided design (CAD) software to create prototypes of new designs prior to ever building them. An even bigger driver of GPU computing has been the consumer video game industry, which has seen price and performance trends similar to the rest of the consumer computing industry. The relentless drive to higher performance at lower cost has given the average user unheard-of performance both on the CPU and the GPU.

Three-dimensional graphics processing must process millions or billions of 3D triangles in 3D scenes multiple times per second to create animation. Placing and coloring all of these triangles in their 3D environment requires a huge number of very similar calculations. Initially, 3D graphics were done using a fixed rendering pipeline, which took the 3D scene information and turned it into pixels that could be presented to the user in a video or on the screen. This fixed pipeline was implemented in hardware, with various parts of the GPU doing different pieces of the problem of turning triangles into pixels. In the early 2000s, this fixed pipeline was gradually replaced by generalized software shaders, which were miniprograms that performed the operations of the earlier fixed hardware pipeline.

With these shaders, high-performance computing folks noticed that the floating-point coordinates and colors could look an awful lot like physics or chemistry problems if you looked at them just right. The more hardcore hacker types started creating graphics problems that looked a lot like nonsense except that the underlying calculations being done solved hard problems remarkably fast. The performance gains got noticed, and computing frameworks, which used the GPUs for doing nongraphics calculations, were developed. These calculations are the same type needed for data mining.

GPUs are a green field. Historically the ability to develop code to run on the GPU was restrictive and costly. Those programming interfaces for developing software that takes advantage of GPUs have improved greatly in the last few years. Software has only started to take advantage of the GPU, and it will be several years before the computations needed for data mining are efficiently delegated to the GPU for execution. When that time comes, the speedup in many types of data mining problems will be reduced from hours to minutes and from minutes to seconds.

MEMORY

Memory, or random access memory (RAM) as it is commonly referred to, is the crucial and often undervalued component in building a data mining platform. Memory is the intermediary between the storage of data and the processing of mathematical operations that are performed by the CPU. Memory is volatile, which means that if it loses power, the data stored in it is lost.

In the 1980s and 1990s, the development of data mining algorithms was very constrained by both memory and CPU. The memory constraint was due to the 32-bit operating systems, which allow only 4 GB of memory to be addressed. This limit effectively meant that no data mining problem that required more than 4 GB of memory[2] (minus the software and operating system running on the machine) could be done using memory alone. This is very significant because the data throughput of memory is typically 12 to 30 GB/sec, and the fastest storage is only around 6 GB/sec with most storage throughput being much less.

Around 2004, commodity hardware (Intel and AMD) supported 64-bit computing. At the same time operating systems became capable of supporting larger amounts of memory, the actual price of memory dropped dramatically. In 2000, the average price of 1 MB of RAM was $1.12. In 2005, the average price was $0.185; and in 2010, it was $0.0122.

With this support of 64-bit computing systems that can address up to 8 TB of memory and the drop in memory prices, it was now possible to build data mining platforms that could store the entire data mining problem in memory. This in turn produced results in a fraction of the time.

Data mining algorithms often require all data and computation to be done in memory. Without external storage, the increase in virtual and real address space as well as the dramatic drop in the price of memory created an opportunity to solve many data mining problems that previously were not feasible.

To illustrate this example, consider a predictive modeling problem that uses a neural network algorithm. The neural network will perform an iterative optimization to find the best model. For each iteration, it will have to read the data one time. It is not uncommon for neural networks to make thousands of passes through the data to find

---

[2] The largest integer value that 32-bit operating systems can use to address or reference memory is $2^{32}-1$, or 3.73 GB, of memory.

the optimal solution. If these passes are done in memory at 20 GB/sec versus on disk at 1 GB/sec, a problem that is only 10 seconds to solve in memory will be more than 3 minutes to solve using disk. If this scenario is repeated often, the productivity of the data miner plummets. In addition to the productivity of the human capital, if the data mining processes relied on disk storage, the computation would take many times longer to complete. The longer a process takes to complete, the higher the probability of some sort of hardware failure. These types of failure are typically unrecoverable, and the entire process must be restarted.

Memory speeds have increased at a much more moderate rate than processor speeds. Memory speeds have increased by 10 times compared to processor speeds, which have increased 10,000 times. Disk storage throughput has been growing at an even slower rate than memory. As a result, data mining algorithms predominantly maintain all data structures in memory and have moved to distributed computing to increase both computation and memory capacity. Memory bandwidth is typically in the 12 to 30 GB/sec range, and memory is very inexpensive. High-bandwidth storage maxes out in the 6 GB/sec range and is extremely expensive. It is much less expensive to deploy a set of commodity systems with healthy amounts of memory than to purchase expensive high-speed disk storage systems.

Today's modern server systems typically come loaded with between 64 GB and 256 GB of memory. To get fast results, the sizing of memory must be considered.

NETWORK

The network is the only hardware component that is always external to the computer.[3] It is the mechanism for computers to communicate to other computers. The many protocols and standards for network communication will not be discussed here beyond the very limited details in this section.

The network speed should be a factor only for a distributed computing environment. In the case of a single computer (workstation or

---

[3] Storage can sometimes be external in a storage area network (SAN).

server), the data, memory, and CPU should all be local, and performance of your analytical task will be unaffected by network speeds.

The standard network connection for an analytical computing
cluster is 10 gigabit Ethernet (10 GbE), which has an upper-bound
data transfer rate of 4 gigabytes per second (GB/sec). This data transfer
rate is far slower than any of the other essential elements that have
been discussed. Proprietary protocols like Infiniband® give better data
throughput but still do not match the speed of the other components.
For this reason, it is very important to minimize usage of the network
for data movement or even nonessential communication between the
different nodes in the computing appliance.

It is this network speed bottleneck that makes parallelization of a
number of the data mining algorithms so challenging. Considerable
skill in the software infrastructure, algorithm selection, and final implementation is required to fit a model efficiently and precisely using
one of many algorithms while not moving any data and limiting communication between computers.

The network speed of your high-performance data mining platform
will be important if you have a distributed computing environment.
Because the network data transfer rate is much slower than other components, you must consider the network component when evaluating
data mining software solutions.

CHAPTER **2**

Distributed Systems

I f you look back before electronic computers, the term "computer" meant a person who performed numerical calculations. Because roomfuls of these computers were in use for most of human history, arguably distributed (i.e., multiperson) computing dates back much farther than conventionally asserted.

Modern distributed computing arguably derives from the 1990s efforts to build "Beowulf" clusters of computers and from early ad hoc computing.[1] Beowulf clusters of computers were standard server or even desktop computers that were networked. The software on the computers then communicated closely with each other over the network to split the work to be done across the computers. Early ad hoc computing efforts, including distributed.net and SETI@Home, used idle home computers to search for cryptography keys and alien radio signals in radio astronomy data. Neither of these projects had the computing power in-house to solve the problem, nor sufficient budget to do it. However, the problems were simple enough that a large number

---

[1] I tried with limited success to build a Beowulf cluster in the late 1990s with cast-off computers.

of computers could make considerable progress with minimal coordination between them. Home computers running the distributed.net or SETI@Home software contacted the main server to get a chunk of work to be done (keys to check or radio signal data to examine).

Classical supercomputers were very large, very expensive machines that contained specialized fast hardware and processors. These supercomputers had contained in their specialized hardware features such as multiple central processing units and vector hardware. Vector hardware is used to perform identical operations on multiple pieces of data. For instance, a two-dimensional vector has components X and Y. Adding a set of vectors is done by components, so providing a single instruction that adds both X and Y simultaneously can result in doubling processing speed.

The cost of hardware has dropped dramatically. Both high-core/large-memory (massively parallel processing [MPP] systems) and clusters of moderate systems allow much larger data mining projects to be feasible. For big data analytics, the only solution is to move the analytics to the data; it is impractical to move the data to the analytics because of the time required for the data transfer.

Harder problems—problems that consume much larger volumes of data, with much higher numbers of variables—may now be considered for analysis. Cluster computing can be divided into two main groups of distributed computing systems. The first is the database, which has been a fixture in data centers for decades. The second is the distributed file system, which is currently dominated by Hadoop.

DATABASE COMPUTING

The relational database management system (RDBMS) or simply database has been around since the 1970s and until recently has been the most common place to store data generated by organizations. A number of huge vendors as well as open source projects provide database systems. Traditional RDBMSs are designed to support databases that are much larger than the memory or storage available on a single computer. From those early days, there are now a number of different databases that serve special purposes for organizations around high-performance data mining and big data analytics.

In-memory databases (IMDBs) were developed starting in the 1990s. IMDBs are now a popular solution used to accelerate mission-critical data transactions for finance, e-commerce, social media, information technology, and other industries. The idea behind IMDB technology is straightforward—holding data in memory and not on disk increases performance. However, there are notable drawbacks to IMDBs, namely the increased cost and volatility of memory.

MPP (massively parallel processing) databases began to evolve from traditional DBMS technologies in the 1980s. MPP databases are meant to serve many of the same operational, transactional, and analytic purposes as the previous generation of commercial databases but offer performance, availability, and scalability features designed to handle large volumes of data while utilizing standard user interfaces. MPP databases are positioned as the most direct update for organizational enterprise data warehouses (EDWs). The technology behind MPP databases usually involves clusters of commodity or specialized servers that hold data on multiple hard disks.

A big advantage of database computing is the time saved in moving the data to the analytics. In a truly big data problem, the time to move the data and the hardware resources needed to process it efficiently once it is moved make the strategy inefficient. Using software that can move the analytics to the data and process it in place leveraging the large computational resources that a distributed database provides will lead to faster models and shorter run times when compared to nondistributed computing systems.

FILE SYSTEM COMPUTING

There are many options in choosing a platform for file system computing, but the market is rapidly consolidating on Hadoop with its many distributions and tools that are compatible with its file system, such as Hive, MapReduce, and HBase.

Hadoop was created by Doug Cutting and Mike Cafarella. (See Figure 2.1.) The name "Hadoop" is not an acronym or a reference to anything really. It came from the name that Cutting's son had given to a stuffed yellow elephant. It was initially developed in 2004 based on the work Cutting and Cafarella had done on Nutch[2] and a paper published by Google that introduced the MapReduce paradigm for processing data on large clusters. In 2008, Hadoop had become a top-level Apache project and was being used by several large data companies such as Yahoo!, Facebook, and *The New York Times*.

A current trend is to store all available data in Hadoop. Hadoop is attractive because it can store and manage very large volumes of data on commodity hardware and can expand easily by adding hardware resources with incremental cost. Traditionally, systems were sized based on expected volumes of data, without the expectation that data would accumulate in perpetuity. Hadoop has made large-scale accumulation of data feasible and potentially is a significant differentiator for competitive advantage. Those who can exploit the value of historical data successfully can gain a huge advantage in the future.

Hadoop is becoming the front-runner for housing large volumes of historical data. However, this data is rarely (actually probably never) in an appropriate form for data mining.

Also, for many problems, other data repositories are used to augment the data in Hadoop. For example, credit card transactions may be stored in Hadoop, but the cardholder account information may be

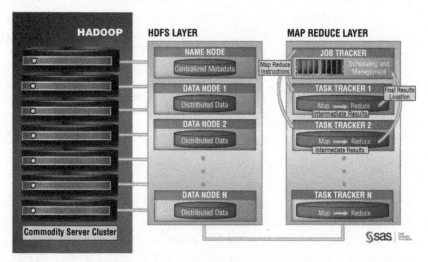

Figure 2.1 Graphical illustration of a Hadoop System

---

[2] Nutch is an Apache open source web crawling project.

stored and maintained in a traditional database. The data survey step includes identifying the data and the data repositories that will be used in the modeling process. Then the data must be combined, summarized, and stored for data mining. This work normally will be done in Hadoop because the computational cost per unit is lower than MPP or RDBMS. This hybrid approach to storing data is likely to be common practice for many years until either Hadoop matures to the level of databases or another technology emerges that makes both databases and Hadoop less desirable.

Cloud computing, because it is able to rapidly provision new servers or to bring down servers no longer needed, can be used in either capacity. However, not all of the high-end tweaks, such as specialized networking hardware, are available. Their flexibility allows one to rapidly change between simple ad hoc computing and coordinated computing and even to mix the models on the fly.

CONSIDERATIONS

Here are some questions to consider as you consider your high-performance data mining platform.

- What is the size of your data now?
- What is the anticipated growth rate of your data in the next few years?
- Is the data you are storing mostly structured data or unstructured data?
- What data movement will be required to complete your data mining projects?
- What percentage of your data mining projects can be solved on a single machine?
- Is your data mining software a good match for the computing environment you are designing?
- What are your users' biggest complaints about the current system?

Figure 2.2 compares a number of big data technologies. The figure highlights the different types of systems and their comparative strengths

	In-Memory Database	MPP Database	Big Data Appliance	Hadoop	NoSQL Database
Consistent	●	●	●	▲	▲
Available	●	●	●	▲	▲
Fault tolerant	●	●	▲	●	●
Suitable for real-time transactions	●	●	●	◆	◆
Suitable for analytics	▲	▲	●	●	◆
Suitable for extremely big data	◆	▲	▲	●	●
Suitable for unstructured data	◆	◆	▲	●	●

Figure 2.2 Comparison of Big Data Technologies

and weaknesses. The purchasing decision for the data mining computing platform will likely be made by the IT organization, but it must first understand the problems being solved now and the problems that are needed to be solved in the near future. The consideration of platform trade-offs and the needs of the organization, all shared in a transparent way, will lead to the best outcome for the entire organization and the individual stakeholders.

In Figure 2.2 the symbols have the following meaning:

- Circle: Meets widely held expectations.
- Triangle: Potentially meets widely held expectations.
- Diamond: Fails to meet widely held expectations

Big data/data mining projects must address how data moves through the entire end-to-end process.

The computing environment is critical to success: Your computing environment comprises four important resources to consider: network, disk, central processing units (CPUs), and memory. Time to solution goals, expected data volumes, and budget will direct your decisions regarding computation resources. Appropriate computing platforms for data analysis depend on many dimensions, primarily the volume of data (initial, working set, and output data volumes), the pattern of access to the data, and the algorithm for analysis. These will vary depending on the phase of the data analysis.

CHAPTER **3**

Analytical Tools

*Information is the oil of the 21st century, and analytics is
the combustion engine.*

—Peter Sondergaard

When faced with a business challenge, people need tools to overcome issues and find ways to create value. In the analytics forum, frequently that begins very early on with deciding what tool should be used. This is the third consideration before work is begun. The first two, where to store the data and how to prepare it for analysis, were discussed in Chapters 1 and 2. This chapter details some tools that are commonly used. Some I have great familiarity with and, in fact, contributed to their development. Others I have used as tools, just as you or your teams will, and a few I have not used personally, but they also should be considered. I have tried to provide a balanced assessment of the strengths and weakness of each tool.

WEKA

Weka (Waikato Environment for Knowledge Analysis) is an open source data mining offering, fully implemented in Java, and primarily developed at the University of Waikato, New Zealand. Weka is notable for its broad range of extremely advanced training algorithms, its work flow graphical user interface (GUI), and its incorporation of data visualization tools. Weka allows users access to its sophisticated data mining routines through a GUI designed for productive data analysis, a command line interface, and a Java application programming interface (API). However, Weka does not scale well for big data analytics, as it is limited to available RAM resources, typically on one machine. Users with 64-bit operating systems will have access to much larger RAM resources, but Weka's documentation directs users to its data preprocessing and filtering algorithms to sample big data before analysis. As many of the most powerful algorithms available in Weka are unavailable in other environments without custom software development, sampling may be the best practice for use cases necessitating Weka. In recent releases, Weka has made strides toward multithreading and simple multitasking. In Weka 3.6, some classifiers can train models on multiple cross-validation folds simultaneously, and the Weka server deployment allows for running data mining tasks concurrently on one machine or a cluster. Weka routines also provide advanced analytics components for two Java-based big data analysis environments: Pentaho and MOA (Massive Online Analysis).

Weka is a good option for people who may not have Java programming experience and need to get started quickly to prove value. I used Weka during a survey course in graduate school about data mining tools. It was a few years after Weka was completely rewritten to use Java. The interface provided big productivity gains for me, because I was not a very experienced Java programmer. I was able to analyze data with far less start-up investment in the programming language.

JAVA AND JVM LANGUAGES

For organizations looking to design custom analytics platforms from scratch, Java and several other languages that run on the Java Virtual Machine (JVM) are common choices. For large, concurrent, and networked applications, Java presents considerable development advantages over lower-level languages, without excessive performance sacrifices, especially in the realm of big data analytics. While languages that execute directly on native hardware, particularly FORTRAN and C, continue to outperform Java in RAM and CPU-bound calculations, technological advances in the Java platform have brought its performance nearly in line with native languages for input/output and network-bound processes, like those at the core of many open source big data applications. Probably the most recognizable Java-based big data environment, Apache Hadoop, beat out several other technologies in the 2008 and 2009 TeraByte Sort Benchmark. It was the first Java-based technology to win the well-respected bench marking contest.

Java's advantages and disadvantages as a general-purpose programming language have been widely discussed in many forums, and will be addressed only briefly here. Developers of analytic applications often avoided Java in the past, because the exhaustive runtime library was unnecessary for numerical routines and the memory management by the JVM platform caused unacceptable slowdowns, to name just two reasons. As analytic applications grew dramatically in scale and complexity, development time became a more serious concern, and memory and CPU-bound performance became less so. In the specific context of building data mining applications, Java's strengths arise from its development efficiency: its rich libraries, many application frameworks, inherent support for concurrency and network communications, and a preexisting open source code base for data mining functionality, such as the Mahout and Weka libraries. Although at some cost to performance, development advantages also stem from the JVM platform. In addition to portability, the JVM provides memory management, memory profiling, and automated exception handling.

Scala and Clojure are newer languages that also run on the JVM and are used for data mining applications. Scala is an open source language developed in Switzerland at the École Polytechnique Fédédale de Lausanne. It was first released in 2003 and aims to be an improvement on Java.

Scala is used to construct data mining applications because it encompasses the development efficiencies of Java—through interoperability with the Java Runtime Environment—and adds functional programming, all with a more concise syntax. Scala allows developers to switch between functional programming and object-oriented (OO) programming paradigms, whereas Java's grammar and syntax tend to enforce

OO design. Functional languages are regarded positively for data mining applications because they handle memory differently from OO and procedural languages. For instance, a major concern in procedural and OO multithreaded applications is preventing multiple threads from changing the same variable at the same time. Functional programming languages avoid this by never changing variables. Even though it is a less common programming paradigm, functional programming is a valuable tool that should not be discounted. Scala is gaining in popularity and has been used to implement major open source projects like Akka and Spark. Akka is a toolkit for building large, parallel, and distributed applications on the JVM, and Spark is a high-performance data mining environment from the University of California Berkeley AMP Lab. Scala is also used commercially for various purposes by FourSquare, the Guardian, LinkedIn, Novell, Siemens, Sony, Twitter, and others.

Clojure was written by Rich Hickey and released in 2007. It is a functional programming language and a dialect of the Lisp programming language, with additional scripting and concurrency features. Although not designed specifically for big data applications, these intrinsic characteristics make Clojure an excellent candidate for building data analysis software. Clojure defaults to immutable data structures, removing an entire category of thread safety design concerns as compared to procedural and OO languages. Clojure treats data in a very holistic manner, presenting developers many convenient ways to process its comprehensive set of data structures and inheriting the concept of code as data from Lisp. This approach to sequences of data eliminates another class of common programming errors related to boundary conditions, specifically in comparison to C and FORTRAN. Clojure also inherits its simple syntax, lazy evaluation, and highly effective macro facility from Lisp. The macro facility allows for the creation of domain-specific languages (DSLs), and DSLs for SQL (ClojureQL) and Hadoop (Cascalog) integration have already been established. When Clojure's unique strengths are combined with those of the JVM platform and access to Java libraries, it becomes a formidable general-purpose programming asset. The first adopters of Clojure have generally been smaller, technologically or analytically advanced companies and start-ups. However, larger corporations and institutions, such as Citigroup and the Max Planck Institute, have reported using Clojure as well.

R

R is an open source fourth-generation programming language designed for statistical analysis. R grew from the commercial S language, which was developed at Bell Laboratories starting in the late 1970s. R was ported from S and SPLUS—another commercial implementation now licensed by TIBCO—by researchers at the University of Auckland, New Zealand, and first appeared in 1996.

R is very popular in the academic community, where I was first exposed to it. I used it to experiment with new analysis that I didn't have time or expertise to code myself and to complete homework assignments. At the time the software also had wonderful graphing functionality superior to others I had used. I leveraged this graphing facility in graduate school and while working at the U.S. Census Bureau. Although these graphing facilities are still present in R, it has lost its competitive advantage to other software.

R has grown to a position of prominence in the broad and growing data science community, enjoying wide usage in academic settings and increasing acceptance in the private sector. Large companies, such as Bank of America, Google, Intercontinental Hotels, Merck, Pfizer and Shell, are known to use R for a variety of purposes. The September 2013 TIOBE general survey of programming languages put R in 18th place in overall development language popularity, far outranking S and S-SPLUS, and in close proximity to commercial solutions like SAS (at 21st) and MATLAB (at 19th) (TIOBE, 2013).[1] R is also extremely customizable. There are thousands of extensions for R, up from about 1,600 in 2009. Extension packages incorporate everything from speech analysis, to genomic science, to text mining into R's baseline analysis functionality. R also boasts impressive graphics, free and polished integrated development environments (IDEs), programmatic access to and from many general-purpose languages, interfaces with popular proprietary analytics solutions including MATLAB and SAS, and even commercial support from Revolution Analytics.

---

[1] The TIOBE programming community index is a measure of popularity of programming languages, calculated from a number of search engine results for queries containing the name of the language.

R is experiencing a rapid growth in popularity and functionality, and many of the memory issues that made dealing with larger data difficult in previous versions of R have been resolved. Significant development work is currently under way to circumvent remaining memory limitations through cluster computing and interfaces to Hadoop. R's short update cycle has made this work available to R consumers through official packages like snow, multicore, and parallel, and younger projects like RHadoop and RHIPE. Aside from Rhadoop and RHIPE, these packages are not meant for true big data analysis but for CPU- and memory-intensive calculations of the "embarrassingly parallel" variety, often executed through R's lapply() construct, where a function is applied to all the elements of a list.

Snow is used to run R calculations on a cluster of computers. It uses sockets, MPI, PVM or NetWorkSpaces to communicate between cluster nodes.[2] The snow package employs traditional master-worker parallelization architecture, holds results in memory on the master node, and requires arguments to snow function calls to fit in memory. Thus, being memory bound, the package is used primarily for CPU-intensive computations, such as simulations, bootstrapping, and certain machine learning algorithms.

Multicore is a simple-to-install-and-implement package that splits sequential R processes running on a single POSIX-compliant machine (OS X, Linux, or UNIX) into a multithreaded process on the same machine. Processes executed simultaneously using multicore are limited to single-machine RAM and other shared memory constraints.

Parallel is a parallel execution package that comes standard in R 2.14 and higher. It expands out-of-the-box parallel execution to the cluster level for POSIX-compliant operating systems and to the multiprocessor level for Windows. Parallel shares a great deal of syntax,

---

[2] PVM (Parallel Virtual Machine) is a software package that permits a heterogeneous collection of Unix and/or Windows computers connected together by a network to be used as a single large parallel computer. Thus, large computational problems can be solved more cost effectively by using the aggregate power and memory of many computers. The software is very portable. NetWorkSpaces (NWS) is a powerful, open source software package that makes it easy to use clusters from within scripting languages like Matlab, Python, and R. While these scripting languages are powerful and flexible development tools, their inherent ease of use can, in many cases, cause natural limitations.

functionality, and limitations with both snow and multicore, and can use snow cluster objects.

Rhadoop and **Rhipe** allow programmatic access to Hadoop, using the R language. Map and reduce tasks can be run from R on a Hadoop cluster.

PYTHON

From its inception in the late 1980s, Python was designed to be an extensible, high-level language with a large standard library and a simple, expressive syntax. Python can be used interactively or programmatically, and it is often deployed for scripting, numerical analysis, and OO general-purpose and Web application development. Python is an interpreted language and typically performs computationally intensive tasks slower than native, compiled languages and JVM languages. However, Python programs can call compiled, native FORTRAN, C and C++ binaries at run time through several documented APIs. Python programs can be multithreaded, and like JVM languages, the Python platform conducts memory management and exception handling, relieving the developer from that responsibility. The Python language has also been ported to the JVM platform, in a project called Jython.

Python's general programming strengths combined with its many database, mathematical, and graphics libraries make it a good fit for projects in the data exploration and data mining problem domains. Python's inherent file handling and text manipulation capabilities, along with its ability to connect with most SQL and NoSQL databases, allow Python programs to load and process raw and tabular data with relative ease. Mathematical and statistical models can be implemented using the Scipy and Numpy libraries, which have strong support for linear algebra, numerical analysis, and statistical operations. Newer Python libraries, like Orange and Pattern, provide high-level data mining APIs, and the Matplotlib library can generate complex and nuanced data visualizations. Python can also be used to write map and reduce directives for MapReduce jobs using the Hadoop Streaming utility.

Python recently has become much more used in the data mining and data science communities with the maturity of the scikit-learn toolkit. The toolkit is currently on release 0.14 but offers a number of useful algorithms and manipulation techniques. Python's scikit does not have any user interface beyond the programming IDE, which allows users flexibility but makes the initial learning curve steep and decreases productivity for routine tasks.

SAS

SAS is the leading analytical software on the market. In the 2013 IDC report ("Worldwide Business Analytics Software"), SAS not only had a significant market share but held more market share than the next 16 vendors combined. The SAS System was first sold in 1976, and two of the four cofounders are still active in the company—Dr. Jim Goodnight and John Sall. The SAS System is divided into a number of product areas including statistics, operations research, data management, engines for accessing data, and business intelligence (BI). For the topic of this book, the most relevant products are SAS/STAT®, SAS® Enterprise Miner™, and the SAS text analytics suite. SAS has been rated as the leading vendor in predictive modeling and data mining by the most recent Forrester Wave and Gartner Magic Quadrant. These ratings reveal the breadth and depth of the capability of the software. In my experience, there is no analytical challenge that I have not been able to accomplish with SAS. Having worked for the company for almost a decade, I have a much better understanding of the meticulous work and dedication of the development team and the tremendous lengths they go to ensure software quality, meet customer requests, and anticipate customers' future needs.

The SAS system is divided into two main areas: procedures to perform an analysis and the fourth-generation language that allows users to manipulate data. This is known as the DATA Step.

One of the unique achievements of SAS is the backward compatibility that is maintained release after release. I saw this firsthand at the U.S. Census Bureau. We had several SAS programs that were well over 15 years old, and they provided the same verifiable results with each update to SAS. This was essential because frequently the original author of the computer programs had moved on to other departments or in some cases no longer worked at the Census Bureau.

SAS uses a comprehensive scheme to provide the best computational performance while being flexible to individual customer environments. The procedure, or PROC as it is commonly referred to, is a module built for a specific analysis, like the REG procedure for building regression models or the UNIVARIATE procedure for doing descriptive statistics on a single variable. In a simple example, let us take a task of computing a mean for a given variable.

This can be trivially accomplished in any programing language because the mean is simple: $\sum_1^n i/n$. This can be computed in the data step with code like this:

```
Data a;
      Set b end=last;
Retain x;
Sum+x;
If last then mean=sum/_n_;
Run;
```

This example shows where a new data set that will be created from data set b. The retain statement tells SAS to keep the values when moving to a new observation (row); the if statement tells SAS that if this is the last observation in the data set, divide the sum by the number of observations, which is stored in the automatic variable _n_. This code is not difficult to write and explain, but there is an alternative approach that is better for SAS users:

```
Proc means data=b;
      Var x;
Run;
```

Besides being shorter, this code is also easier to read, uses code written for a specific purpose instead of general-purpose code, and I did not need to make a copy of the data just to add one new column. The procedure also handles and documents a number of behaviors that become very important when you develop your own software (e.g., working with ties, missing values, or other data quality issues). SAS has 82 procedures in the SAS/STAT product alone. Literally hundreds of procedures perform specific analyses. A major advantage of SAS over other software packages is the documentation. SAS/STAT has over 9,300 pages of documentation and Enterprise Miner has over 2,000 pages.

The SAS system processes data in memory when possible and then uses system page files to manage the data at any size efficiently. In the last few years, SAS has made major changes in its architecture to take better advantage of the processing power and falling price per FLOP (floating point operations per second) of modern computing clusters.

PART
TWO

Turning Data into
Business Value

This second part of the book shifts from the storage of data, preparation of data, hardware considerations, and the software tools needed to perform data mining to the methodology, algorithms, and approaches that can be applied to your data mining activities. This includes a proven method for effective data mining in the sEMMA approach, discussion about the different types of predictive modeling target models, and understanding which methods and techniques are required to handle that data effectively. From my experience, most business environments use several people to perform each of the tasks. In larger organizations, the tasks might be split across many groups and organizationally only meet at the executive level of the organization. A quote from Shakespeare that I have always appreciated to introduce this topic is:

> *If you can look into the seeds of time, And say which grain will grow and which will not, Speak then to me, who neither beg nor fear Your favours nor your hate.*
>
> —*Macbeth*, Act 1, Scene 3

This verse shows an appreciation and understanding from hundreds of years ago that those people who can predict future behavior have a distinct advantage regardless of the venue. In sports, this is often call field presence: the talent some players have to effectively anticipate where the ball will be played and be there before the ball arrives. On Wall Street, fortunes are won by correctly anticipating the movement of the market in advance. In your business, correctly anticipating customer behavior or reducing future expenditures has a real impact. The goal in this section is to explain a methodology for predictive modeling. This process has been in place for over a decade and proven useful for thousands and thousands of users. I also discuss how this methodology applies in the big data era, which reduces or makes optional the need for data sampling.

Part Two discusses the types of target models, their characteristics, and information about their specific uses in business.

In addition, I discuss a number of predictive modeling techniques to help you understand the fundamental ideas behind these techniques, their origins, how they differ, and some of their drawbacks.

Finally, I present a set of methods that you might be less familiar with that address more modern methods for analysis or analysis on specific types of data.

CHAPTER **4**

Predictive
Modeling

*I never guess. It is a capital mistake to theorize before
one has data. Insensibly one begins to twist facts to suit
theories, instead of theories to suit facts.*

—Sir Arthur Conan Doyle,
author of Sherlock Holmes stories

redictive modeling is one of the most common data mining tasks.
As the name implies, it is the process of taking historical data (the
past), identifying patterns in the data that are seen though some
methodology (the model), and then using the model to make predictions about what will happen in the future (scoring new data).

Data mining is a composite discipline that overlaps other branches of science. In Figure 4.1, we can see the contributions of many
different fields in the development of the science of data mining.
Because of the contributions of many disciplines, staying up to date
on the progress being made in the field of data mining is a continuous educational challenge. In this section I discuss algorithms
that come primarily from statistics and machine learning. These two
groups largely live in different university departments (statistics and

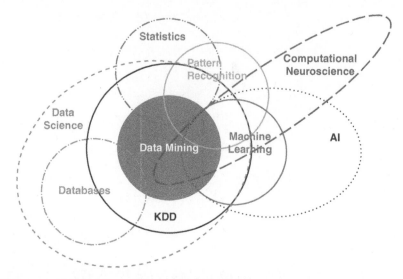

Figure 4.1 Multidisciplinary Nature of Data Mining
Source: SAS Enterprise Miner Training material from 1998.

computer science respectively) and in my opinion are feuding about the best way to prepare students for the field of data science. Statistics departments teach a great deal of theory but produce students with limited programming skills. Computer science departments produce great programmers with a solid understanding of how computer languages interact with computer hardware but have limited training on how to analyze data. This gap requires organizations to train new hires in these areas. There is a recent trend to give students a more complete education and better prepare them to contribute immediately in a data mining role. Until these programs build up their student bases, job applicants will likely know only half of the algorithms commonly used for modeling. For statisticians, that is regression, General Linear Models (GLMs), and decision trees. For the computer scientist, it is neural networks, support vector machines, and Bayesian methods.

Predictive modeling is not necessarily complicated or difficult; it is a fundamental task that we learn at an early age and hone as we grow and gain experience. In your daily life, you inherently do this many times a day. For instance, how long will your afternoon commute be?

My most variable commute has been living in the Washington, DC, area. The important factors in my commute time were these:

- The time I left the office
- The day of the week
- The season (was it summertime?)

Unless you work from home, your commute probably has similar key variables and perhaps a few more that were not important in my commute. Another prediction you make each day is what the weather will be. My children constantly want to wear shorts and T-shirts later into the fall season than social convention dictates. This year after the daily discussion about what the temperature might be during lunch, recess, PE, and the walk to and from school, my wife and I made a firm rule that after Veteran's Day (November 11), pants and long-sleeve shirts were required. Looking at average temperatures, it would have been reasonable to assume that the temperature would not rise to the point of "needing" to wear shorts, but looking at averages is sometimes not a good prediction technique. In the first week of December, while it was 30 degrees in Los Angeles, it was 75 degrees in Cary, North Carolina.

This short story illustrates a number of key points about predictive modeling:

- Sometimes models are wrong.
- The farther your time horizon, the more uncertainty there is.
- Averages (or averaging techniques) do not predict extreme values.

George Box was a pioneer and influential statistician (also the son-in-law of Sir R. A. Fischer) who taught at the University of Wisconsin. In 1987, he published a book titled *Empirical Model Building and Response Surfaces*. In it he makes two statements now famous in the statistical community related to the quality of predictive models. He says: "Remember that all models are wrong; the practical question is how wrong do they have to be to not be useful." Later in the same text he says: "Essentially, all models are wrong but some are useful." These points are important to keep in mind as you use increasing amounts of data to make more specific predictions. Logic and reason should not be ignored because of a model result. Following a developed methodology and using clear processes will help reduce error and allow you to improve processes when things go wrong.

Building on the weather analogy, it is clear that for a stable process, predicting something immediate is more certain than farther out. The weather prediction for tomorrow is more likely to be accurate than the one for five or ten days into the future. The same is true for other stable processes like the stock market, real estate home prices, or gasoline. In statistical terms, this is referred to as a prediction interval, and it becomes larger the farther time horizon you predict for.

This chapter explains a methodology for building predictive models that has been used by thousands and thousands of data miners. After the methodology is developed, you are presented with information about the types of predictive models and their commonality and distinction.

A METHODOLOGY FOR BUILDING MODELS

The process of building models has been developed and refined by many practitioners over many years. Here is a simple, proven approach to building successful and profitable models.

1. **Prepare the data.** This step has to be completed before any meaningful exploration or analysis can take place.

   In larger organizations, this is done by a separate team and perhaps even a different business unit. Regardless of how your data is prepared, either through a formal request and accompanying specifications, as I did at the U.S. Census Bureau, or if you have permission to query directly from the enterprise data warehouse (EDW), this step is essential to a successful model.

   Investment in understanding the data preparation process within your organization often pays benefits in the long run. As you need access to increasingly larger and more granular data, knowledge of what data exists and how it can be combined to other data sources will provide insight that was not possible just a few years ago. If your IT organization is not keeping more data for longer and at finer levels, then you are behind the trend and at risk for becoming irrelevant in your market.

2. **Perform exploratory data analysis.** This is the step where you understand your data and begin to gain intuition about relationships between variables. This exploration is best done with a domain expert, if you do not have that expertise. Fantastic data miners will discover relationships and trends through complicated exploration. They will, with great excitement, present these findings to a domain expert who will politely reply that those things have been known for some time. You cannot give a complete and thorough analysis and recommendation in today's business climate without domain expertise to complement analytical skill.

The tools used for exploratory data analysis have changed in the past few years. In the late 1990s, this was done using mostly tabular output by means of SQL or a scripting language. There were correlation matrix and static graphical output to be pored over. The work was often slow, and programming skills were a requirement. In the last few years, the graphical tools have improved dramatically. There are now many commercial products from SAS, IBM, and SAP, as well as smaller vendors like QlikTech, and Tableau, to name a few, in the space of business visualization. These products are able to load data for visual exploration, generally through a browser-based interface, and provide a highly interactive experience in exploring data. This technology has been proven to work with billions of observations, assuming sufficient hardware resources are available.

The exploration of data is never complete. There are always more ways to look at the data and interactions and relationships to consider, so the principle of sufficiency and the law of diminishing returns need to be observed. The law of diminishing returns comes from the field of economics and states that adding one more unit of effort (time in our case) will yield less increased value per unit for each successive unit of effort you put into the task. In this case, the insight and knowledge you gain between hours 15 and 16 on data exploration is most likely less than the insight you gained between hours 2 and 3. The principle of sufficiency acknowledges the law of diminishing returns and sets a threshold on productivity loss. Stated in common language, this is: Know when to stop exploration. The software development methodology has moved to incorporate this idea through agile processes of learning a little, getting started, and continuous improvement.

3. **Build your first model.** The key for this step is to realize up front that the successful model-building process will involve many iterations. During some projects, the Thomas Edison quote that "I have not failed. I've just found 10,000 ways that won't work" will seem very apt. Until you build the first model, you are not able to accurately evaluate what the potential impact of the model will be. Build this model quickly with a method you are most comfortable with. (I frequently use a decision tree.) Building the first model helps to cement the criteria for success and set appropriate expectations for the people who will use the model predictions. Human nature is to be optimistic. We think products will sell better than they do, jobs will be completed without complications, and so on. Building the first model is a reality check for future performance and expectations. This first model is, by default, the champion model.

4. **Iteratively build models.** This phase is the where the majority of time should be spent. This step is a feedback loop where you will build a model (the challenger) and then compare it to the champion model using some objective criteria that defines the best model. If the challenger is better than the champion model, then evaluate if the challenger model satisfies the project objectives. If the project objectives are not met or the champion is not displaced then build another model. Often there is not a concrete model evaluation to determine when to stop but rather a time window that forces the project to end. Say you are contracted to provide a list of customers for a marketing

campaign. The campaign has a deadline for providing the customer list for next Tuesday, so model building will continue until that point in time.

sEMMA

sEMMA is a data mining methodology, created by SAS, that focuses on logical organization of the model development phase of data mining projects. It describes the process one must go through to capture insight and knowledge from their data. The acronym sEMMA—sample, explore, modify, model, assess—refers to the core process of conducting data mining. Beginning with a statistically representative sample of your data, sEMMA makes it easy to apply exploratory statistical and visualization techniques, select and transform the most significant predictive variables, model the variables to predict outcomes, and confirm a model's accuracy.

Before examining each stage of sEMMA, let us address a common misconception. A common misunderstanding is to refer to sEMMA as a data mining methodology. sEMMA is not a data mining methodology but rather a logical organization of the functional tool set of SAS Enterprise Miner for carrying out the core tasks of data mining. Enterprise Miner can be used as part of any iterative data mining methodology adopted by the client. Naturally, steps such as formulating a well-defined business or research problem and assembling quality representative data sources are critical to the overall success of any data mining project. sEMMA is focused on the model development aspects of data mining:

Sample (optional) your data by extracting a portion of a large data set. This must be big enough to contain the significant information, yet small enough to manipulate quickly. For optimal cost and performance, SAS Institute advocates a sampling strategy that applies a reliable, statistically representative sample of large full-detail data sources. Mining a representative sample instead of the whole volume reduces the processing time required to get crucial business information. If general patterns appear in the data as a whole, these will be traceable in a representative sample. If a niche is so tiny that it is not represented in a sample, and yet so important that it influences the big picture, it can be discovered using summary methods. We also advocate creating partitioned data sets with the Data Partition node:

- Training—used for model fitting.
- Validation—used for assessment and to prevent overfitting.
- Test—used to obtain an honest assessment of how well a model generalizes.

Explore your data by searching for unanticipated trends and anomalies in order to gain understanding and ideas. Exploration helps refine the discovery process. If visual exploration does not reveal clear trends, you can explore the data through statistical techniques including factor analysis, correspondence analysis, and clustering. For example, in data mining for a direct mail campaign, clustering might reveal groups of customers with distinct ordering patterns. Knowing these patterns creates opportunities for personalized mailings or promotions.

Modify your data by creating, selecting, and transforming the variables to focus the model selection process. Based on your discoveries in the exploration phase, you may need to manipulate your data to include information, such as the grouping of customers and significant subgroups, or to introduce new variables. You may also need to look for outliers and reduce the number of variables to narrow them down to the most significant ones. You may also need to modify data when the "mined" data change either due to new data becoming available or newly discovered data errors. Because data mining is a dynamic, iterative process, you can update data mining methods or models when new information is available.

Model your data by allowing the software to search automatically for a combination of data that reliably predicts a desired outcome. Modeling techniques in data mining include neural networks, tree-based models, logistic models, and other statistical models—such as time series analysis, memory-based reasoning, and principal components. Each type of model has particular strengths and is appropriate within specific data mining situations depending on the data. For example, neural networks are very good at fitting highly complex nonlinear relationships.

Assess your data by evaluating the usefulness and reliability of the findings from the data mining process, and estimate how well it performs. A common means of assessing a model is to apply it to a portion of data set aside during the sampling stage. If the model is valid, it should work for this reserved sample as well as for the sample used to construct the model. Similarly, you can test the model against known data. For example, if you know which customers in a file had high retention rates and your model predicts retention, you can check to see whether the model selects these customers accurately. In addition, practical applications of the model, such as partial mailings in a direct mail campaign, help prove its validity.

By assessing the results gained from each stage of the sEMMA process, you can determine how to model new questions raised by the previous results and thus proceed back to the exploration phase for additional refinement of the data.

Once you have developed the champion model using the sEMMA-based mining approach, it then needs to be deployed to score new customer cases. Model deployment is the end result of data mining—the final phase in which the return on investment from the mining process is realized. Enterprise Miner automates the deployment phase by supplying scoring code in SAS, C, Java, and PMML. It not only captures the code for analytic models but also captures the code for preprocessing activities. You can seamlessly score your production data on a different machine and deploy the scoring code in batch or real time on the Web or directly in relational databases. This results in faster implementation and frees you to spend more time evaluating existing models and developing new ones.

sEMMA for the Big Data Era

How is sEMMA methodology impacted in the era of big data? The short answer is that largely it is not. sEMMA is a logical process that can be followed regardless of data size or complexity. However, the 's,' or sample, in sEMMA is less likely to be as critical with the more powerful systems available for mining the data. From my experience in working with big data, very large analytical databases can be addressed using sEMMA.

BINARY CLASSIFICATION

From my experience, binary classification is the most common type of predictive model. Key decision makers for corporations and other organizations must often make critical decisions quickly, requiring a system to arrive at a yes/no decision with confidence. These systems are not designed to do things part way or with some likelihood. They either do them or they do not. This is illustrated very well in the famous "go or no go for launch" checklist that each system's flight controller must answer. A launch can proceed only after the flight director has run through each system and received the "go for launch" answer. In the business world, many decisions are binary, such as should I extend you credit for this car purchase, or will you respond to this marketing campaign.

With predictive modeling of a binary target, the probability that an event will or will not occur is also very useful information. Let me provide an example to illustrate this point. With a binary target we are creating a black-and-white situation; will it rain tomorrow—yes or no? It will either rain or it will not, but you are very unlikely to see your local meteorologist (or even the National Weather Service) give a chance of rain at 0% or 100% because while it will either rain (100%) or not rain (0%), the estimate is implicitly the degree of confidence we have in our prediction. This confidence estimate is often much more useful than the binary prediction itself. Does your behavior differ if you see a 10% chance of rain versus a 40% chance of rain? Are you willing to leave your windows down or the top off of your convertible? Both of these predictions, because the percentage is less than 50, indicate that it is less likely to rain than not. However, from experience with having wet car seats for my commute home from a day when it was unlikely to rain (30%), I keep my windows up if there is *any* chance of rain because the downside risk is much greater than the potential upside.

An often-seen case in binary predictive modeling is when you are dealing with a "rare event." What qualifies as a rare event differs depending on the industry and domain, but it universally means that the event happens with extremely low probability and therefore might require some special treatment in the analysis.

Using an example from the sport of golf, let us examine the rare event more closely.[1] The most sought-after event in golf is the hole in one. This is where a golfer takes a tee shot during at least a 9-hole round and makes it in the hole in one shot. If you make a hole in one during some tournaments, you can often win a car, and custom dictates that regardless of when it happens, you buy a round of drinks for everyone in the clubhouse.[2] To be official, the shot must be witnessed by someone else. The United States Golf Association (USGA) keeps a registry of all holes in one and estimates the odds of hitting a hole in one to be 1 in 33,000. So while the odds of anyone hitting a hole in one is very small (.003%), some people, like Tiger Woods, not only have hit one but hit multiple holes in one. Tiger has 18 recorded holes in one but does not lead in this category. The most holes in one recorded goes to Norman Manley, with 59. To put quantitative terms around the odds of hitting a hole in one, we would say that no one is likely to hit a hole in one. Assuming 1 in 33,000 tee shots results in a hole in one and (after removing long holes) that there are 14 holes you could reasonably make a hole in one on, if you golfed a round every day of the year you would, on average, hit a hole in one every seven years.

Once we have determined the probability of the event occurring for each observation, they are then sorted in descending order from largest probability to smallest probability based on the likelihood the event will occur. Using the example above, if we were marketing commemorative hole-in-one plaques, we would apply the model to all golfers in our database sorting the list from highest probability to lowest probability of making a hole in one. We would then mail an offer letter to all the golfers from the top of the list down until our marketing campaign budget is exhausted or to those who exceeded a certain threshold. This will ensure that we send the offer for a commemorative plaque to the golfers, based on the model, most likely to hit a hole in one and who would be interested in our services.

---

[1] For full disclosure, I golfed a lot growing up but never hit a hole in one. I'm now in retirement since I haven't played a round of golf since my oldest child was born.

[2] Did you know that you can purchase hole-in-one insurance? Policies start at few hundred dollars depending on the prize offered during the tournament.

MULTILEVEL CLASSIFICATION

Multilevel or nominal classification is very similar to binary classification with the exception that there are now more than two levels. Nominal classification is an extension of binary classification. There are several examples where nominal classification is common, but for the most part this is the rarest of targets. An example of such a model can be seen in the cell phone industry when looking at customer churn. A company may notionly be interested in the binary response of whether an account remains active or not. Instead, it may want to dive deeper and look at a nominal response of voluntary churn (customer chooses to cancel the contract), involuntary churn (e.g., contract was terminated due to delinquent payments), or an active customer.

In many cases, a nominal classification problem arises when an exception case is added to what could be a binary decision. This happens in the case of preventing credit card fraud, for example. When a credit card transaction is initiated, the card issuer has a very short window to accept or decline the transaction. While this could be thought of as a simple binary problem, accept or decline, there are some transactions in which the decision is not that straightforward and may fall into a gray area. A third level of response may be added to indicate that this transaction needs further review before a decision to accept or decline can be made.

The nominal classification problem poses some additional complications from a computational and also reporting perspective. Instead of just computing one probability of event (P) and then taking $1 - P$ to arrive at the probability of nonevent, you need to compute the probability of event #1 (P_1), the probability of event #2 (P_2), and so on until the last level which can be computed using $1 - \sum_{i=1}^{n-1} P$. There is also a challenge in computing the misclassification rate. Since there are many choices, the report values must be calibrated to be easily interpreted by the report reader.

INTERVAL PREDICTION

The final type of prediction is interval prediction, which is used when the target level is continuous on the number line. Salary is an example of a prediction that employers and employees alike would like to make accurately. The property and casualty insurance industry is an area with many interval prediction models. If you own a car in the United States, you are required to have insurance for it. To get that insurance, you likely requested a quote from several different insurance companies, and each one gave you a slightly different price. That price discrepancy is due to different predictive models and business factors that each insurance company uses. The business factors are the amount of exposure in certain geographic markets or an overall directive to try to gain market share in a certain market either geographic or economic strata.

Companies in the insurance industry generally utilize three different types of interval predictive models including claim frequency, severity, and pure premium. The insurance company will make predictions for each of these models based on its historical data and your specific information including the car make and model, your annual driving mileage, your past history with driving infractions, and so on.

ASSESSMENT OF PREDICTIVE MODELS

One consideration in the process of building predictive models will be to determine which model is best. A model is comprised of all the transformations, imputations, variable selection, variable binning, and so on manipulations that are applied to the data in addition to the chosen algorithm and its associated parameters. The large number of options and combinations makes a brute-force "try everything" method infeasible for any practical data mining problem. So the issue of model assessment plays an important role is selecting the best model. Model assessment, stated simply, is trying to find the best model for your application to the given data. The complexity comes from the term "best." Just like purchasing a washing machine, there are a number of aspects to consider and not everyone agrees on a single definition of "best." The common set of model assessment measures are listed and defined next. As an example, consider a local charity that is organizing a food drive. It has a donor mailing list of 125,000 people and data from past campaigns that it will use to train the model. We partition the data so that 100,000 people are in the training partition and 25,000 are in the validation partition. Both partitions have a response rate of 10%. The validation partition will be used for assessment, which is a best practice.

Table 4.1 Decision Matrix for Model Assessment

	Predicted Nonevent	Predicted Event
Nonevent	True negative	False positive
Event	False negative	True positive

Classification

There are a set of assessment measures that are based on the 2×2 decision matrix as shown in Table 4.1.

Classification is a popular method because it is easy to explain, it closely aligns with what most people associate at the "best" model, and it measures the model fit across all values. If the proportion of events and nonevents are not approximately equal, then the values need to be adjusted for making proper decisions. (See Table 4.2.)

Receiver Operating Characteristic

The receiver operating characteristics (ROC) are calculated for all points and displayed graphically for interpretation. The axis of the ROC plot are the Sensitivity and 1-Specificity, which were calculated from the classification rates.

Table 4.2 Formulas to Calculate Different Classification Measures

Measure	Formula
Classification rate (accuracy)	$\dfrac{true\ negative + true\ positive}{total\ observations} \times 100$
Misclassification rate	$(1 - \dfrac{true\ negative + true\ positive}{total\ observations}) \times 100$
Sensitivity (true positive rate)	$\dfrac{true\ positive}{true\ positive + false\ negative} \times 100$
Specificity (true negative rate)	$\dfrac{true\ negative}{false\ positive + true\ negative} \times 100$
1-Specificity (false positive rate)	$\dfrac{false\ positive}{false\ positive + true\ negative} \times 100$

Lift

Lift is the ratio of percentage of correct responders to percentage of baseline response. To calculate lift, it must be accompanied by a percentile in the data. This is commonly referred to as a depth of file, and usually the first or second decile is chosen. For the food drive example, if we compute the lift at the first decile (10% of the data), the baseline (or random) model should have 2,500 responders to the campaign so that in the first decile there will be 250 responders (2,500×.1). Our model is good; it captures 300 responders in the first decile so the lift at the first decile is 1.2 (300/2500=12% captured response/10% baseline response). I prefer to use cumulative lift for my model assessment because it is monotonic and in practice campaigns will sort a list by the likelihood to respond and then market until a natural break is observed or the budget for the campaign is exhausted.

Gain

Gain is very similar to lift except 1 is subtracted from the value $\dfrac{\% \ of \ model \ events}{\% \ of \ baseline \ events} - 1$ for a given decile. For the food drive example, the gain would be 0.2 at the first decile.

Akaike's Information Criterion

Akaike's information criterion (AIC) is a statistical measure of the goodness of fit for a particular model. It maximizes the expression $-2(LL + k)$ where

k = number of estimated parameters (for linear regression the number of terms in the mode)

LL = maximized value of the log-likelihood function for the given model

The smaller the AIC, the better the model fits the data. Because of the k term, the smaller number of model parameters are favored. AIC values can be negative, but I do not remember ever encountering that in a real-world data mining problem.

Bayesian Information Criterion

The Bayesian information criterion (BIC) is a statistical measure similar to AIC but that maximizes the expression $-2LL + k \times \ln(n)$ where:

n = number of observations (or sample size)

k = number of estimated parameters (for linear regression the number of terms in the mode)

LL = maximized value of the log-likelihood function for the given model

For any two given models, the one with the lower BIC is better. This is because the number of terms in the model is smaller, the variables in the model better explain the variation of the target, or both.

Kolmogorov-Smirnov

The Kolmogorov-Smirnov (KS) statistic shows the point of maximum separation of the model sensitivity and the baseline on the ROC curve.

Model assessment is ideally done on a holdout partition that is representative of the data but was not used in the model-building phase. This holdout partition (often called a validation or test partition) is essential to measure how well your model will generalize to new incoming data.

CHAPTER **5**

Common Predictive Modeling Techniques

The key part of data mining and in my opinion the most fun is after the data has been prepared and the data scientist is able to conduct a "model tournament." Because of the complexity and size of most modern data mining problems, the best practice is to try a number of different modeling techniques or algorithms and a number of attempts within a particular algorithm using different settings or parameters. The reason for so many trials is that there is an element of brute force that needs to be exerted to arrive at the best answer. The number of iterations needed to achieve the best model can vary widely depending on the domain and the specific modeling challenge.

---

*The data analysis for this chapter was generated using SAS Enterprise Miner software, Version 13.1 of the SAS System for Windows. Copyright © 2013 SAS Institute Inc. SAS and all other SAS Institute Inc. product or service names are registered trademarks or trademarks of SAS Institute Inc., Cary, NC, USA.

It is important to note that while this chapter is focused on predictive modeling or supervised learning, many of these techniques can be used in unsupervised approaches to identify the hidden structure of a set of data. Supervised learning has a target variable, and the methods attempt to correctly classify or predict as many of the observations as possible. Supervised learning has clear measures and assessment as to the model quality. In contrast, unsupervised learning lacks a target and therefore strong objectiveness as to measure model quality.

Each of the following sections covers a different modeling technique and has the general progression of brief history on the technique, a simple example or story to illustrate how the method can be used followed by a high-level mathematical approach to the method and finally a references section for you to get additional details.

Finally, in this chapter, many of the most popular predictive modeling techniques are discussed with examples, graphics, and some mathematical details. This is designed to give you an overview of the techniques and their uses.

RFM

RFM, or recency, frequency, and monetary modeling, is a very simple but effective way to rank customers. It looks at how long since a customer's last visit (recency), how often they purchase (frequency), or how much they spend (monetary). This method is desirable because it does not require sophisticated software or knowledge of "fancy" algorithms. The method can be easily explained to all levels of management and domain knowledge. The method is most common in database marketing or direct marketing. A basic approach is to take each metric and divide them into segments. These might be data driven, such as the deciles of how much households spend, or they might be rule driven, such as recency of 0–90 days, 91–180 days, and 181+ days, to align with common accounting practices. If we take the simple example of just two levels in each dimension, then we will have eight segments as shown in Table 5.1. The number of segments can be generally computed using:

$$Levels_{Recency} \times Levels_{Frequency} \times Levels_{Monetary}$$

Table 5.1 RFM Segmentation with Two Groups per Variable

Segment	Recency	Frequency	Monetary
1	2	2	2
2	1	2	2
3	2	1	2
4	1	1	2
5	2	2	1
6	1	2	1
7	2	1	1
8	1	1	1

All customers will fall into one of these segments. By segmenting the customers, you can design a specific campaign or treatment to help maximize profits. Looking at the segments from Table 5.1, it is clear that segment 1 is the most valuable set of customers. They have recently made a purchase, they frequently purchase, and they spend an above average amount compared to your average customer.

Using the segment assignments from Table 5.1, it is clear that segment 1 is the most valuable and segment 8 is the least. However, there is less clarity in the other segments, and it is common in practice to profile the segments and perhaps combine some if there are not sufficient differences.

The typical RFM segmentation is to use five bins, one for each quintile, per factor for a total of 125 segments. It is advisable not to use the RFM method for prediction because while it is accurate under many circumstances, it is only a historical measure. It has no ability to account for changes in macroeconomic factors or individual life transitions, such as birth, death, divorce, or retirement, which would drastically modify your marketing strategy.

A couple of differences between RFM and the other techniques in this section are that RFM does not produce any type of score code that can be applied to new observations. This is in contrast to the other methods, such as decision trees, where a main output is to deploy the model into a production system that will very quickly score incoming records or could be used to score a large customer table. In the case of RFM, the whole process must be repeated when new data is added to the data set. Another distinction is because of the lack of score code and repeating of the process, scores cannot be compared across data sets. If you look at the 555 group (which denotes the best of the best customers in a typical setting) from a consumer retail scenario for December sales, that will likely be a very different set of customers with different profiles and different qualifications than the customers from May sales. The number of sales, their amounts, and their frequency are very different for the Christmas holiday season versus May.

There are two main strategies to using the RFM scores, and they vary depending on if you feel that recency is more important than frequency, which is more important than monetary. If that is the case, then a simple sorting of the data will allow targeting the most important clients, and you can continue sequentially through the list until your campaign budget is exhausted. The rationale for believing that recency is most important is that the longer it takes for your customers to return to your business, the less likely they are to ever return. It is easier to affect the customer behavior of how often they come or how much they spend, but a greater time since the last contact increases that chance that you have already lost that high-value customer. Alternatively, if you do not feel that constraint applies perhaps because of a variety of reasons, then a score of 345, 534, or 453 are all roughly equal and so you can sum the individual digits of the score (12) in this case and sort the list by the summed score beginning with the customers receiving a 15 and moving down the list until the campaign budget is exhausted. A number of variations on this method can also be applied to add some level of sophistication, such as secondary sorts or multiplying the individual scores (R,F, or M) by a weighting factor to reflect the relative importance of each.

A last consideration that is needed for RFM and for many of the modeling techniques is the data preparation before the technique can be applied. In a retail setting, the sales database is full of transactions that have relatively few details: typically just date, time, account number, store ID, and amount. There will typically be a transaction ID that will link to a different table in the enterprise data warehouse that includes a full list of the shopping cart. But all of this data is transactional, and RFM needs customer-level data so an extract, transform, and load (ETL) process (which was discussed earlier in Part One) to create that data set is summarized at the customer level.

This method is largely based on the Pareto principle, which is commonly explained as the 80/20 rule. It describes that 80% of your revenue comes from just 20% of your customers. The name comes from an observation by the Italian economist Vilfredo Pareto in 1906 that 80% of Italy's land was owned by only 20% of the population. This also led to the Pareto distribution, which is a power distribution and has applications in many observable phenomena in the social and actuarial fields, among others.

REGRESSION

Regression analysis is likely the first predictive modeling method you learned as a practitioner during your academic studies or the most common modeling method for your analytics group. Regression concepts were first published in the early 1800s by Adrien-Marie Legrendre and Carl Gauss. Legrendre was born into a wealthy French family and contributed to a number of advances in the fields of mathematics and statistics. Gauss, in contrast, was born to a poor family in Germany. Gauss was a child math prodigy but throughout his life he was reluctant to publish any work that he felt was not above criticism. After his death, many of his personal journals were discovered that detailed his ideas and thoughts. Those ideas were significant advances in the field of mathematics. It is estimated that if Gauss had been more aggressive in publishing his work, he could have advanced the field of mathematics more than 50 years. Those two brilliant men along with Sir R.A. Fischer in the early twentieth century describe the method of regression.

The term "regression" was coined by Francis Galton (who was a cousin of Charles Darwin) to describe the biologic process of extreme values moving toward a population mean. A common example of this is children of tall (above-average height) parents "regressing" toward the mean of the population and being shorter than their parents; conversely children of short (below-average height) parents being taller than their parents. Prior to Galton, the technique was referred to as "least squares."

From my experience, regression is the most dominant force in driving business decisions today. Regression analysis has many useful characteristics; one is the easy interpretation of results. Regression concepts are widely understood, and the methodology is well developed such that a well-tuned regression model by a skilled practitioner can outperform many algorithms that are gaining popularity from the machine learning discipline.

Basic Example of Ordinary Least Squares

As an example, let us look at the relationship of weight and height for a class of 19 middle school students. There is an expected and natural relationship, a positive correlation, between weight and height where we expect students who weigh more to be taller. Let us first show a plot of weight and height to see what that relationship looks like (Figure 5.1).

As you can see in Figure 5.1, there is a trend that the more you weigh, the taller you are, but there is in no way a perfect relationship.

To begin, let us consider the question of interest. We want to find a line that best predicts the height of a student knowing his/her weight, as in the next equation.

$$H_i = \beta_0 + W_i \beta_1$$

where

H_i = height of an individual student

W_i = weight of an individual student

β_0 = intercept

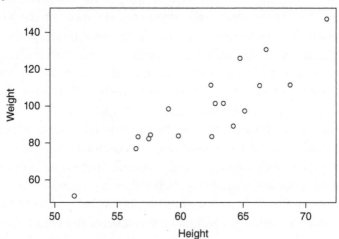

Figure 5.1 Scatter Plot for Height and Weight for Class

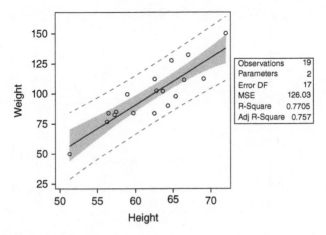

Observations	19
Parameters	2
Error DF	17
MSE	126.03
R-Square	0.7705
Adj R-Square	0.757

Figure 5.2 Fit Plot for Weight

In regression analysis, the best line is the one that minimizes the sum of error across all data points. The error for an observation is measured as the squared distance between the proposed line, which is the predicted value, and the open circle, which is the actual value. Why is the vertical distance between the point and the line squared? Because with points above the line and other points below the line, a simple adding of the distance between the points will result in an infinite number of lines that will give us a summed value of 0. But using the square of the distance there is a single best line that gives us the minimum sum of the squares. This statistic is called the sum of squares, and this is a very useful measure of how well the regression line fits the data. You can see the best regression line in Figure 5.2.

In addition to the calculation of the sum of squares to find the best-fitting line, a number of diagnostics need to be considered as part of performing a regression analysis.

The residual plot is the single most important plot to review before accepting the prediction from a regression model. A proper residual plot will look like a random scatter of points (like the one shown in Figure 5.3).

If you see a funnel shape where the points start close to the reference line near 0 on the X-axis and then spread out as they move to

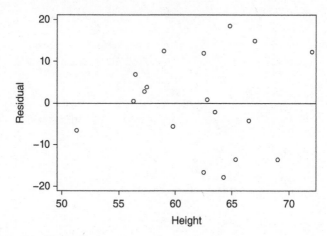

Figure 5.3 Residuals for Weight

the right, variable transformations are needed for your input variables. (See Figure 5.4.)

If the points have consistent spread but form a curve in either direction (a happy face or sad face), such as Figure 5.5, then you need to transform your input variables. The Box-Cox transformation method can often be used to find a transformation to improve the fit of your model in this scenario.

The diagnostic plots shown in Figure 5.6 present a great deal of information. Here is a brief explanation for several of the key diagnostic plots.

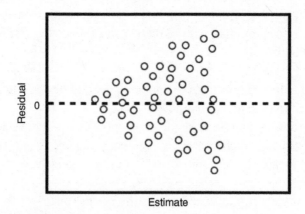

Figure 5.4 Plot Residuals in a Funnel Shape

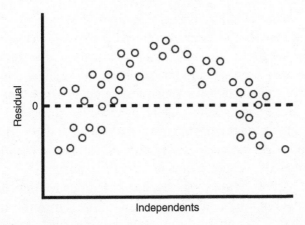

Figure 5.5 Residuals in an Arc

Beginning with the upper left and moving across the first row in Figure 5.6:

> The residual plot has already been discussed, but additionally it shows the fit of the errors to the data. It is an essential plot to assess model fit and a residual plot where the points appear random is the ideal plot.

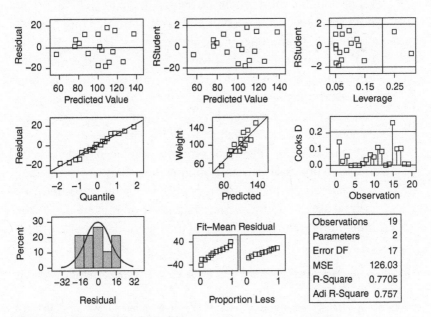

Figure 5.6 Fit Diagnostics for Weight

The studentized[1] residuals show the same pattern as the residuals, but the variables have been first studentized, which is analogous to normalizing or standardizing. For this example, because there is only one variable, the residual and studentized residual plots look identical except for the Y-axis range. If there are multiple independent variables, then the process of studentizing them will ensure that variables with larger values and larger variances do not dominate the model fitting, which could reduce model quality.

The leverage plot examines the influence that each individual point has on the regression line. Since the technique is trying to minimize the distance of the sum of squares that are at the extremes of the range of observations (either very small or very large), they have more influence on the line than the points in the center. You can think of this middle of the range like the seesaw from the playground from your youth. The farther from the center of the seesaw, the less force (weight) is needed to lift the other side. This is similar to your data. A small set of points or even a single point can alter the regression line substantially, as shown in Figure 5.7. The single outlier moves the regression line away from the very good fit of the line to the data if the outlier is not present. You can deal with outliers in several ways. One option is to remove the observation after some investigation to ensure there is some reasonable justification. Because often this is not possible or cost effective in working with big data, another option is to use a robust regression technique and winsorize[2] the observations.

Quantile plot (Figure 5.6 second row left plot) is used to assess quantiles of two distributions to each other; in this case the comparison is that the residuals are being compared to a normal distribution. The more points are on the line $X = Y$, the more normal the residuals are. If the points made an "S" shape,

---

[1] William Gosset, who wrote several papers under the pseudonym Student, developed this method.

[2] Winsorize is a statistical transformation to limit extreme values. It was invented by a biostatistician named Charles Winsor.

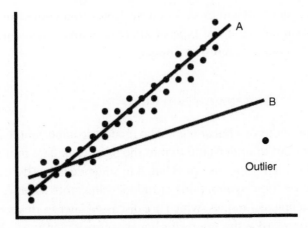

Figure 5.7 Effect of Outlier on Regression Line

that would indicate more probability in the tails. If only one side moves away from the line, that likely indicates outliers or skewness of the distribution.

Predicted versus actual plot show how well the regression line predicted the values for a set of observations with known outcomes.

Cook's D plot is also used for outlier detection. By looking at the Cook's D value, you can determine the relative influence each observation had in the fitting of the regression line.

Percentile versus residual is another view to express the same information as the QQ plot.

R-Square (R^2) is a simple transformation of taking the studentized residuals and squaring the terms. This has the productive properties of making all the terms positive and helping to scale them to be more in line with human intuition. The scale is also now conveniently bounded between 0 and 1 as opposed to –1 and 1.

The power of regression analysis is the ability to describe the relationship between a dependent, label, or target variable[3] and a set

---

[3] These are all terms to describe the same thing. The discipline of the practitioner largely determines the vocabulary used.

of independent attributes or input variables. Depending on the dependent variable and the type of analysis, many techniques can be deployed to build a regression model.

Assumptions of Regression Models

The assumptions of a linear regression model are important to note. It is also important to understand that in the practice of data mining, some if not all the assumptions are violated to some degree. There are ways to overcome these assumptions including using more advanced regression modeling techniques, which are discussed later in this section.

The standard assumptions for linear regression are:

- There is no measurement error in the observed values of the target and each input variable. Basically it is assumed that the values in the data set are correct.
- The relationship between the dependent variable and all of the independent variables are linear.
- The observations are independent.
- The independent variables are not linear combinations of each other.
- The variance of the dependent variable is constant (homoscedasticity)

For logistic regression, there is an additional assumption:

- The true conditional probabilities are a logistic function of the independent variables.

Additional Regression Techniques

Here is a list of advanced regression techniques that are useful in data mining with large data. Observations will be more extreme and relationships between variables more complex.

- Adaptive regression fits multivariate adaptive regression spline models. This is a nonparametric regression technique that combines both regression splines and model selection methods.

This regression technique can use both continuous and discrete inputs.

■ Generalized additive models (GAM) are nonparametric, meaning that they do not require the assumption of linear predictors. GAMs produce smooth functions of the regression variables. This technique is most useful in fitting additive models for non-normal data. The technique can use both continuous and discrete inputs.

■ Locally estimated scatterplot smoothing (LOESS) uses a local regression method to fit nonparametric models. This method is good for modeling data from an unknown distribution, and outliers are likely to be present in the data.

■ Orthogonal regression uses the Gentleman-Givens computational method to perform regression on ill-conditioned data. The Gentleman-Givens method often provides more accurate parameter estimates and nonspecialized regression methods.

■ Partial least squares regression, in addition to finding the minimal prediction error for a response variable, also balances that with the variation of the predictor or input variables. This balance is often achieved by using linear combinations of variables like those found in principle components.

■ Proportional hazards regression uses the Cox models to fit regression models to survival data.

■ Quantile regression is used to model the effects of covariates on the conditional quantiles of a response variable.

■ Robust regression uses Huber M estimation and high breakdown value estimation to fit models. This regression method is good for detecting outliers and providing stable predictions when the data contains outliers.

Applications in the Big Data Era

Regression analysis is a fundamental predictive modeling method to a student of statistics, but it is potentially a new and innovative idea for those who come from other disciplines, such as computer science. I was recently watching a talk on machine learning in preparation for a presentation. The speaker, a well-educated practitioner from a prestigious university, said: "We use a method called logistic regression for those of you that are not familiar with it. . ." This was a reminder to me that the area of data mining is very broad and people approach problems from different perspectives.

From my experience working with customers even in the big data era, regression is still the dominant method for predictive modeling. I think that can be attributed to many factors. The first is easy-to-explain output. The parameter estimates that result from a regression analysis are very approachable to people from a wide range of quantitative skill and business knowledge. Second, the results can be used to determine the key factors in the model (sometimes called driver variables or key performance indicators [KPIs]). Third, the methods are parallelized (or should be); they can be used on nearly any size problem.

Regression is still a very actively researched area, and modern techniques of lasso, robust regression, and ridge regression have all advanced the field based on principles developed over 200 years ago. I expect this field to continue to advance and create new inventions as researchers and practitioners alike look for new ways for regression to provide insight to the relationships within data. In this era where data volumes continue to increase and data is combined in more ways and at lower levels of granularity, the need for advanced regression techniques will remain in demand for a long time. Any software package you are considering for dealing with big data should do regression. If not, that is a big red flag.

GENERALIZED LINEAR MODELS

In 1972, statisticians John Nelder and Robert Wedderburn, who worked together at the Rothamsted Experimental Station in England, defined generalized linear models (GLMs) as a unified framework for probit[4] models in pursuit of chemical dosage tolerance, contingency tables, ordinary least squares (OLS) regression, and many more. This generalized

---

[4] Probit is a statistical term that describes a type of regression model that only has two possible values: for example, male or female.

description of models lifted the restrictions, which were prohibitive for certain types of problems, and offered the flexibility to accommodate response variables that are nonnormally distributed, have a mean with a restricted range, and/or have nonconstant variance—which are all violations of the assumptions for OLS regression. GLMs are characterized by three components:

1. The probability distribution of the response variable Y_i (the random component) can be any distribution from the exponential family.[5]
2. The linear model which includes the explanatory variables and the model parameters, $x'_i\beta$ (the systematic component).
3. The link function which describes the relationship between the systematic and random components.

More specifically, the usual linear component of a linear model, $x'_i\beta$, now links to the expected value μ_i of the response variable Y_i through a function g such that $g(\mu_i) = x'_i\beta$. The link function g can be any monotonic, differentiable function.[6] For ordinary linear regression, the link is simply the identity and the response distribution is normal.

A logistic regression model, another example of a GLM, uses the logit link function for the Bernoulli-distributed response variable; in turn, this gives a probability estimate between 0 and 1 for the modeled outcome.[7] This model would be used when the model is trying to predict churn, attrition, or any other binary event where the event of interest is not as important as the likelihood that the event will occur.

---

[5] The exponential family of distribution include normal, gamma, beta, and chi-squared among many others.

[6] "Monotonic" is a property where the values of an independent variable never decrease. "Differentiable" means that there is a derivative that exists at each point along the function.

[7] The Bernoulli distribution is named after Jacob Bernoulli, a Swiss seventeenth-century mathematician. The distribution is one discrete trial (like a coin toss) with probability of success p and probability of failure $q = 1 - p$.

Counts can be modeled in a GLM using a Poisson or negative binomial distribution and a log link function. Examples of count models could include the number of claims someone makes against an insurance policy, the number of cars passing through a toll booth, the number of items that will be returned to a store after purchase, or any other counting-type process where the occurrence of one event is independent from another occurrence.

Example of a Probit GLM

I, like most people, do not like bugs in my home. Because North Carolina has lots of bugs, to keep them out of my house, I spray periodically the perimeter of my home and the trunks of my trees with pesticide. I have a friend whom I met when I first moved to North Carolina who worked for a national pest consumer control company. His job was to research the effectiveness of certain chemical compounds with killing pests. Consider this common example for modeling whether an insect dies from a dosage of a toxic chemical in a pesticide. Several different dosages were applied to a sample of insects, and data was collected on how many insects lived and died at the particular dosages. The plot in Figure 5.8 shows the proportion of insects that died; the Y-axis represents the proportion that died, at certain dosage amounts represented on the X-axis. While the relationship between these two variables does appear somewhat

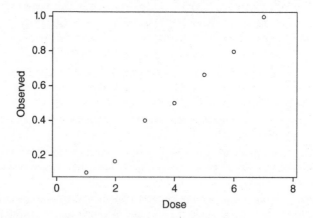

Figure 5.8 Proportion of Response by Dose

linear, a linear regression model is not suitable in this case; we are trying to predict the probability of dying at a particular dosage, which needs to be between 0 and 1 because we cannot have less than 0% of the insects die or more than 100% of the insects live, and OLS is not bounded. This probability of death P at a given dosage or log dosage, x, is equal to the probability that the insect's tolerance for the chemical T is less than x. The tolerance for all subjects (or in this case insects) at a fixed dosage or log dosage is often assumed to have a normal distribution with mean μ and standard deviation σ. Thus we have:

$$P = \Pr(T < x) = \Phi\left[(x - \mu)/\sigma\right]$$

The function Φ is the standard normal cumulative distribution function, and its inverse Φ^{-1} is the probit function. Since Φ^{-1} is a legitimate link function, this model can be expressed in the form of a GLM as:

$$\Phi^{-1}(P) = \beta_0 + \beta_1 x$$

where

$$\beta_0 = -\mu/\sigma$$

$$\beta_1 = 1/\sigma$$

One of the motivations for Nelder and Wedderburn's paper was to introduce a process for fitting GLMs because an exact estimate of the parameters was not available most of the time.[8] They presented an iterative weighted least squares process that can be used to obtain the parameter estimates of β. The predicted probability of death $\hat{p}$ can be estimated from the MLEs of β as:

$$\hat{P} = \Phi\left(\hat{\beta}_0 + \hat{\beta}_1 x\right)$$

Figure 5.9 shows the probit model curve (the solid line) representing the predicted probabilities that is fit to the data collected.

Unlike the regression example, in most cases for GLMs, we do not get a measure like R-Square to determine how well the model fits. Instead of R-Square, there are a set of measures to evaluate model fit.

---

[8] A closed-form solution for the maximum likelihood estimates of the parameters is not available in most cases (an exception being OLS regression).

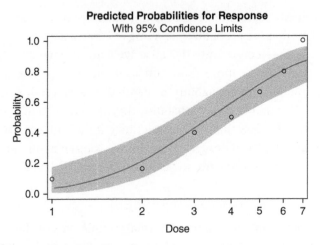

Figure 5.9 Predicted Probabilities for Response

A simple way to classify between the two groups of model fit measures: tests where small values indicate bad model fit and small values indicate good model fit.

For small values are bad:

- Pearson's chi-square statistic
- deviance[9] or scaled deviance

Significant p-values[10] for these two test statistics indicate a lack of fit. For small values are good:

- Akaike information criterion (AIC)
- Corrected AIC (AICC)
- Bayesian information criterion (BIC)

These fit measures can also be used for evaluating the goodness of a model fit, with smaller values indicating a better fit. As for a regression analysis discussed in the Regression section, examining the residual plots can give insight into the reason for a lack of fit, as can other diagnostics mentioned, such as Cook's D for outlier detection.

---

[9] Also called the likelihood ratio chi-square statistic.

[10] p-values are the probability of obtaining a result at least this extreme when the null hypothesis is true.

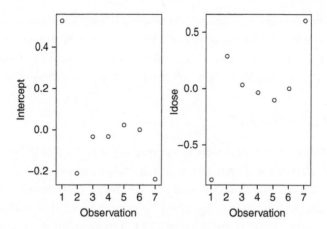

Figure 5.10 Unstandardized DFBETA Plots for Response

The DFBETA and standardized DFBETA statistics are other measures of influence of individual observations on the model fit. An example of the unstandardized DFBETA measure plotted against observation number for each of the two estimated parameters is shown in Figure 5.10. These statistics and plots can help identify observations that could be outliers and are adversely affecting the fit of the model to the data.

Applications in the Big Data Era

A main application of GLMs with respect to big data is in the insurance industry for building ratemaking models. Ratemaking is the determination of insurance premiums based on risk characteristics (that are captured in rating variables); GLMs have become the standard for fitting ratemaking models due to their ability to accommodate all rating variables simultaneously, to remove noise or random effects, to provide diagnostics for the models fit, and to allow for interactions between rating variables. The response variables modeled for ratemaking applications are typically claim counts (the number of claims an individual files) with a Poisson distribution, claim amounts with a gamma distribution, or pure premium models that use the Tweedie distribution. These distributions are all members of the exponential family, and the log link function typically relates the response to a linear combination of rating variables, allowing these models to be formulated as GLMs. One large insurance company based in the United States uses GLMs to build ratemaking models on data that contains 150 million policies and 70 degrees of freedom.

NEURAL NETWORKS

Artificial neural networks were developed in the last half of the twentieth century. They were inspired by a simple mathematical model of a biological neuron—the core structure in the brain that enables learning in animals. In this model, described by neurophysiologist Warren McCulloch and logician Walter Pitts in 1943, a neuron "fires" (i.e., its output becomes 1) when the sum of its excitatory inputs is greater than a threshold value and no inhibitory inputs are 1. McCulloch and Pitts showed that networks of these model neurons could compute the value of most complex logical equations (equations where the variables only have the values 0 or 1). Figure 5.11 is a representation of their original concept.

Starting in the late 1950s, Frank Rosenblatt used a network of neurons similar to McCulloch-Pitts neurons, which he called a perceptron, to correctly identify digitized pictures of letters by weighting the inputs to the neurons and then optimizing those weights using the Perceptron learning algorithm. The Perceptron learning algorithm starts out with a random set of weights and then iteratively modifies those weights based on an error function of the difference between the

Figure 5.11 Original Drawing of a Neural Network
Source: McCulloch, W. S. and Pitts, W. H. (1943). "A logical calculus of the ideas immanent in nervous activity." *Bulletin of Mathematical Biophysics*, 5, 115-133.

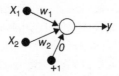

Figure 5.12 Simplified Perception Diagram

actual output of the neuron and the desired output of the neuron (1 if this neuron represents the letter that was digitized and 0 otherwise) for each neuron in the network. This type of training method is now known as supervised learning because it adjusts the weights of the network by looking at a series of examples where the desired output of the network is known. Later, when presented with a set of inputs where the correct output is not known, it is hoped that the "trained" network will output the correct result. (See Figure 5.12.)

Unfortunately, a perceptron can be trained only to classify patterns belonging to linearly separable classes—classes where a hyperplane in the input space can properly separate all patterns, as shown in Figure 5.13.

The lack of ability to model nonlinear relationships in data was pointed out in the book *Perceptrons* by Marvin Minsky and Seymour Papert in 1969. This book became controversial because its analysis of the limitations of perceptrons was interpreted to mean that these limitations would prevent even extended neural networks from solving more complicated, real-world problems. This proved to be false, but this interpretation significantly slowed research into neural networks

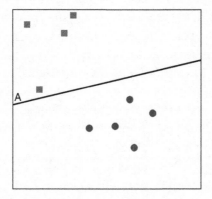

Figure 5.13 Data Properly Separated by a Hyperplane

for more than a decade as research into artificial intelligence shifted away from connectionist algorithms (which represented information as weights and connections) toward symbolic algorithms (which represented information as logical propositions and used logical inference rules to deduce results). An interesting analysis of the controversy over perceptrons is presented by Jordan B. Pollack in his 1989 review of the third edition of *Perceptrons*, "No Harm Intended."

The breakthrough for neural networks came in the latter half of the 1980s after differentiable squashing activation functions (e.g., logistic, tanh, etc.) replaced the nondifferentiable step activation function used in perceptrons. Besides enabling neural networks to model arbitrarily complex functions, the differentiable activation functions enabled the use of the backpropagation method for computing the gradient of the error function with respect to the weights, which in turn enabled the use of the gradient descent algorithm to compute the optimal weights. This method was described in a 1986 paper titled "Learning Representations by Back-Propagating Errors" by David E. Rumelhart, Geoffrey E. Hinton, and Ronald J. Williams.

Finally, in 1989, in reply to the *Perceptrons* book, the paper "Multilayer Feedforward Networks are Universal Approximators" by Kurt Hornik, Maxwell Stinchcombe, and Halbert White, proved that a three-layer (input, hidden, output) neural network, where the hidden layer consisted of neurons with a squashing activajtion function, could "approximate any function of interest to any desired degree of accuracy."

As we sit here in early 2014, neural networks are being used in a wide variety of fields to model everything from credit card fraud, where best to drill an oil well, what stocks to invest in, how to find faces in pictures, whether a person is likely to respond to an ad, whether a person is likely to contract a disease, and whether a drug is likely to cure it.

Despite some of the hype around neural networks, where they are described as "learning" as a human would, they actually represent a straightforward nonlinear regression problem.

In a nonlinear regression problem, a nonlinear function of the input variables is fit by optimizing the weights of a nonlinear function $y(W, X)$

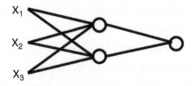

Figure 5.14 Standard Three Layer Neural Network

where

W = weight vector to be computed

X = vector of known input variables

y = known output

A neural network is simply a particular type of nonlinear function, and what is usually seen as a graphical representation is simply a diagram of that function.

The most widely used neural networks are three-layer (input, hidden, and output), feedforward networks using squashing activation functions for the neurons in the hidden layer. Recently neural networks of five or more hidden layers have found to be useful for feature detection in images and in natural language processing.

Figure 5.14 represents the output function $y(Z, W, X) = o(Z \cdot h(W \cdot X))$ where

vector X = input variables

vector W = weights between the input layer and the hidden layer neurons

function h = activation function of the hidden layer neurons

vector Z = weights between the hidden layer neurons and the output layer neurons

function o = activation function of the output layer neurons

Networks like these, generalized to include multiple hidden layers, are referred to as multilayer perceptrons (MLPs). However, the term "neural network" has been applied to a variety of other architectures, such as autoencoders, convolutional neural networks, radial basis function networks (RBF), and self-organizing maps (SOM). The rest of this chapter will focus on multilayer perceptrons.

Multilayer perceptrons are typically used for two types of problems, which usually determines the number of neurons in the output layer, the activation function used by the output layer and the error function used to accumulate the differences between the network output and the desired output.

Regression problems are those where you are trying to predict a numerical value in response to the given input vector (like predicting the age of a person given their weight, height, and sex). Since you are trying to predict a single number, the output layer only contains a single neuron. The identity output activation function is often used for the output layer neuron and the square of the difference between the network output and the desired output is usually used for the error function.

Classification problems are those where you are trying to predict whether a given input vector belongs to one of several classes (like predicting the species of a plant given several of its measurements). Unlike regression problems, where there is a single neuron in the output layer, the output layer usually has one neuron per possible class. The softmax activation function, in combination with the cross-entropy error function, is often used for the output layer neurons because the output value can then be interpreted as the probability that a given input vector belongs to the class represented by each output neuron.

Figure 5.15 represents the two output functions

$$y_1(Z_1, W, X) = o(Z_1 \cdot h(W \cdot X)), \text{ and } y_2(Z_2, W, X) = o(Z_2 \cdot h(W \cdot X))$$

where
vector X = input variables
vector W = weights between the input layer and the hidden layer neurons
function h = activation function of the hidden layer neurons

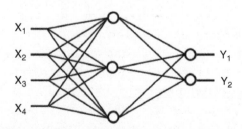

Figure 5.15 Two Output Functions

vector Z_1 = weights between the hidden layer neurons and the first output neuron

vector Z_2 = weight between the hidden layer neurons and the second output neuron

function o = activation function of the output layer neurons

In this example, each output neuron could represent one of two possible classes that each input vector can belong to. The output could be interpreted as: an input vector X belongs to class1 if output y_1 was greater than y_2.

In order to train a neural network, you need a method to compute the weights that will minimize a highly nonlinear objective function for a set of training examples. Remember, the objective function is not the network output—it represents the network error—the total difference between what the network should be outputting and what it is outputting over all training examples.

The task of finding the minimum value of a nonlinear differentiable function is usually accomplished by using some form of either the gradient descent method or Newton's method. Both of these methods require that you repeatedly calculate the gradient of the objective function. In the context of neural networks, the gradient is the vector of partial derivatives of the objective function with respect to each weight. The value of each partial derivative in this vector represents the amount the objective function changes for a small change in weight. The key contribution of the backpropagation algorithm was a straightforward method to efficiently calculate this gradient.

The gradient descent method uses the notion that if you start at randomly chosen initial points (a randomly chosen initial set of weights) and slowly move in the direction of the negative gradient of the objective function (in the steepest downhill direction) you will eventually end up at the bottom, or at least at a place where the gradient is zero (a valley). The reason you have to move slowly is so you don't jump over the actual minimum and have to backtrack. The reason the function has to be differentiable is so the gradient exists, which it does for multilayer perceptrons with standard activation functions, but not, for instance, the step activation function. When using the gradient descent method, you have to decide how far along the negative gradient to move at each step – the step length. One way is to move an amount proportional to the gradient. Here is the formula for the gradient descent method, where

$$W_{n+1} = W_n - \lambda \nabla f(W_n)$$

where

$$W_n = \text{ current vector of weights}$$
$$\lambda = \text{ learning rate}$$
$$\nabla f = \text{ objective function to be minimized}$$

While moving in the direction of the negative gradient provides the steepest descent from the current position, it is not necessarily the direction that gets to the ultimate minimum the fastest.

Newton's method, when used for minimization, uses the first derivative, the gradient, and the second derivative, the curvature, to find the minimum value of a function, and is called a second order method. At each step, it computes a simple quadratic function with the same gradient and curvature as the current objective function, and then finds new weights that would minimize the quadratic function. These new weights will also result in a reduced objective function. It then repeats the process until the gradient of the objective function becomes close to zero. Here is the formula for Newton's method:

$$W_{n+1} = W_n - H^{-1} \nabla f(W_n)$$

where

$$H = \text{Hessian}^{11}$$

Second order methods generally converge to a minimum with far fewer iterations than first order methods like gradient descent, but computation of the inverse Hessian is expensive time-wise, on the order of n^3 operations for a function of n variables (weights). In order to ameliorate this problem, methods that iteratively estimate the inverse Hessian were developed, called Quasi-Newton methods. The most popular of these is probably the BFGS method (Broyden–Fletcher–Goldfarb–Shanno). Like the nonlinear conjugate gradient method, this method first computes a search direction (by multiplying the estimated

---

[11] The Hessian is a matrix of second partial derivatives of the objective function with respect to each pair of weights

inverse Hessian by the current gradient), and then uses an inexact line search along that direction to find a new set of weights, which result in a reduced gradient. However, it still takes n^2 storage locations to store the Hessian. To resolve this last issue, the Limited Memory BFGS (L-BFGS) method was developed.

Some key considerations for working with neural networks are:

- **Starting values.** When the weights of a neural network are near zero, the model is approximated by a linear regression model. Through many iterations the neural network model becomes increasingly nonlinear as the weights change and help define the unobserved nonlinear relationships. If the starting values are too close to zero, then the algorithm fails to converge to the true values. Likewise, starting with large weights usually leads to poor solutions. The challenge is to select starting values that are close enough to zero but do not get stuck there.

- **Overfitting.** One of the biggest worries when using historical data to develop a model that predicts future results is overfitting. Overfitting means the model has been trained to fit a specific set of training observations very well, but does not generalize well—does not do well at predicting the outcomes of observations not used for training. Unlike linear or logistic regression, where you're using historical data to compute just a few model parameters, with neural networks, depending on the number of input variables and number of hidden neurons, you could be fitting your past data with hundreds or even thousands of model parameters (weights). Because neural networks are universal approximators, by adding enough hidden neurons, and running the training algorithm for enough iterations, they will eventually be able to predict the outcomes of the training observations perfectly. But what the neural network is learning during training is the noise in the specific training data set as well as the underlying process that generated the data. When presented with new data, the same noise will not be there.

- **Validation data to adjust for overfitting.** One good answer is to use cross validation during training. You split your training data into a training subset and a validation subset. The validation subset should contain at least 25% of your available data. You must make sure that both subsets have the same distribution of data. You only give the training algorithm the training subset. After each iteration of the training algorithm, you compute the prediction error on both the training and validation subsets, using the current set of weights computed by the training algorithm. What you will typically see is that the error on the training subset (training error) and the error on the validation subset (validation error) both start downward together as the training algorithm does its work. Then, at some point, validation error starts to go up again, even as the training error continues lower. At the point the validation error increases you have achieved your best generalized model.

- **Input scaling.** The scale of the input variables affects the initial weights. It is a best practice to scale the inputs to a mean of 0 and a standard deviation of 1 before beginning to build your model. This will ensure that all input variables are getting fair and equal treatment. The scaling of the input variables also helps identify good starting points.

- **Assurance of global minimum.** Because the goal is to minimize the error is nonconvex (meaning that in hyperspace, any line between two points is not always a valid solution; think of Swiss cheese, where the air bubbles are invalid solutions), it is possible to get stuck at a local minimum and never reach the overall minimum. The ability to find the global minimum is based largely on the starting values.

Basic Example of Neural Networks

Sir Ronald Fisher gathered data on three types of *Iris*. He collected measurements of their petal length, petal width, sepal length, and sepal width. Using these four interval measures, the objective is to correctly classify from these measurements the three species of *Iris*: *virginica*, *versicolor*, and *setosa*.

The first step is to partition the data to make sure that the neural network model does not overfit so we take a stratified sample and split the data 70% for training and 30% for validation. The setup of the

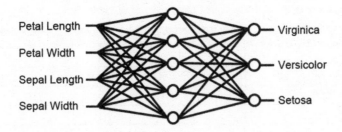

Figure 5.16 Neural Network Diagram for *Iris* Data

network is four input neurons, five hidden neurons, and three target neurons as represented in Figure 5.16.

The initial weights between the input neurons and hidden neurons are randomly initialized. The error term of the objective function is shown in Table 5.2 for 16 iterations.

Table 5.2 Average Error Function (AEF) of Training and Validation for Neural Network for *Iris* Data

Iteration	AEF Training	AEF Validation
0	0.443202	0.443281
1	0.231005	0.244472
2	0.149747	0.178680
3	0.131696	0.158875
4	0.063039	0.070936
5	0.054594	0.075916
6	0.046256	0.063721
7	0.026284	0.028231
8	0.021823	0.020531
9	0.020630	0.018305
10	0.016621	0.015093
11	0.013766	0.014756
12	**0.013696**	**0.014804**
13	0.013559	0.014864
14	0.012273	0.014848
15	0.009394	0.014826
16	0.008228	0.014819

Table 5.3 Comparison of Target and Outcome of *Iris* Validation Data Set

Target	Outcome	Count
SETOSA	SETOSA	15
VERSICOLOR	VERSICOLOR	14
VERSICOLOR	VIRGINICA	1
VIRGINICA	VIRGINICA	15

You can see from the table that the training error continues to shrink as the weights are adjusted and tuned. The validation error, however, begins to rise after the eleventh iteration (shown as bold in Table 5.2). This is because the neural network has now overfit the model to the training data and lost its general predictive power. The model that should be used to classify the *Iris* is the one produced at the eleventh iteration.

The neural network was able to classify all but one observation in the validation data correctly as shown in the third row of Table 5.3 where a virginica iris was mistaken classified as a versicolor iris. This error corresponds to a 2.2% misclassification rate for the validation data.

Recently, the term "deep learning" has become widely used to describe machine learning methods that can learn more abstract concepts, primarily in the areas of image recognition and text processing, than methods previously available. For instance, neural networks with three or more hidden layers have proven to do quite well at tasks such as recognizing handwritten digits (see Figure 5.17), or selecting images with dogs in them.

Training these types of neural networks has proven quite a challenge. The standard backpropagation algorithm begins to fail on networks with large numbers of input variables (each pixel of an image is typically a single input variable) and many hidden layers because the gradient of the total error with respect to the weights in the initial hidden layers becomes extremely small and noisy. This is known as the vanishing gradient problem. In addition, the large number of input variables, which results in very large numbers of weights that must be computed, causes the standard optimization process to be very slow.

In 2006, Geoffrey Hinton and R. R. Salakhutdinov described how they successfully trained seven hidden layer autoencoders (neural networks whose output is trained to be as close to the input as possible) on images using Restricted Boltzmann Machines. In 2010, one of Hinton's

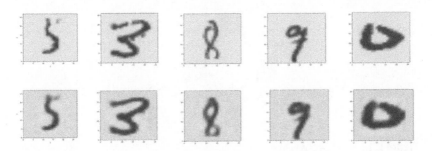

Figure 5.17 Improvement of Digit Recognition Using Deep Learning

graduate students, James Martens, developed a new Quasi-Newton method he called Hessian Free Learning,[11] more accurately described as Truncated Newton Hessian Free Learning, which he claims can also be used to train neural networks with many hidden layers.

DECISION AND REGRESSION TREES

Tree-based methods have long been popular in predictive modeling. Their popularity is owed, in no small part, to their simplicity and predictive power along with the small number of assumptions.

Tree-based methods of modeling have been around since the 1960s, with popular methods including CART, C4.5, and CHAID as common implementations. Decision trees were first presented by Leo Breiman in his 1984 book *Classification and Regression Trees*. The initial CART algorithm has been improved and extended in a number of ways through the years, but the overall principles remain.

Begin with a set of training data and look at the input variables and their corresponding levels to determine the possible split points. Each split point is then evaluated to determine which split is "best." "Best" in this case is creating the purest set of subgroups. The process is then repeated with each subgroup until a stopping condition has been met. The main distinction between decision trees and regression trees is that decision trees assign a category from a finite or nominal list of choices, such as gender or color. Regression trees, in contrast, predict a continuous value for each region, such as income or age.

Consider the problem of trying to predict the gender of students from a general elective course at a university. You could build a decision

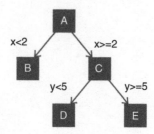

Figure 5.18 Basic Decision Tree

tree that predicts gender by dividing a representative population by height, weight, birth date, last name, or first name. Last name and birth date should have no predictive power. Height and weight, however, would likely be able to predict gender in some cases (the very tall are likely to be male and the very short likely to be female). More predictive still would be first names, as there are fewer names than heights or weights that are gender-neutral. A variable that is hard to capture but probably very predictive is hair length. This example shows that with the right attribute, it is often possible to get near-perfect separation with a single variable. In most real-world problems, that single "magic" variable does not exist, is too costly to collect, or is something that could not be known beforehand for the purposes of scoring new cases.[12]

Decision and regression trees both recursively partition the input space one variable at a time. Often a single split is used at each level, as it is equivalent to multiple splits.

Figure 5.18 shows a tree where the original data set (region A) is first split on variable y by whether it is less than 2 (region B) or greater than or equal to 2 (C). Region C is then further split into two regions, D ($y < 5$) and E ($y >= 5$).

These same regions are shown in Figure 5.19 as partitioned input space. The partitioned input space only shows the leaves of a tree (a leaf is a nodes that have no further splits i.e. terminal node). The leaves that been split are called branches. The branches in Figure 5.19 are A and C.

Building a tree happens in two phases. First, a large tree is created by recursively splitting the input data set using a metric to determine

---

[12] Do not forget that the purpose of building a predictive model is to anticipate a behavior or attribute.

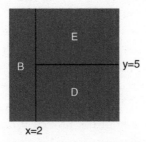

Figure 5.19 Basic Decision Tree Shown as a Partition Region

the best split. Growth continues until a stopping point is reached conditions might include: insufficient data for additional splits, additional
splits do not improve model fit, or tree has reached a specified depth.
After the tree has been built, it is often overfit (which makes it poor for
prediction). That is, it matches the input data too well—it matches all
of the small fluctuations that are present in the input data set but not
in the general population. Thus, the overlarge tree is then pruned back
until it is predictive in general, not just for the particular input data set.
Pruning is particularly effective if a second, validation data set is used
to determine how well the tree performs on general data. This comes
at the cost of taking some data that would have been used to grow the
tree. The C4.5 splitting method attempts to prune based on estimated
error rates instead of using a separate data set.

There are a large number of methods to determine the "goodness"
of a split. A few of the main ones are discussed here—misclassification
rate, entropy, Gini, Chi-square, and variance. The interested reader is
encouraged to consult a survey book, such as *Data Mining with Decision
Trees* by Lior Rokach and Oded Maimon. As they mention, no one
"goodness" method will be the best in every scenario, so there is benefit in being familiar with a number of them.

Consider the *Iris* data that was used as an example in the Neural
Networks section. After the data is portioned using the same 70% for
training and 30% for validation, all the split points from the four input
variables are evaluated to see which gives the purest split. As you can
see in the figure on the next page, if the petal width is less than 7.5 mil-
limeters (mm), then the *Iris* is a *setosa*. If the petal width is greater than
7.5 mm or missing, then it is either *versicolor* or *virginica*. A further split

is needed to create a distinction among all three groups. All of the variables and their split points are then considered for how to refine the group for purity. In this case the petal width is again the best variable to create pure groups. This time the split point is having a petal width of less than 17.5 mm or missing (and greater than 7.5 mm because those observations have already been removed). About 90% of those *Iris* are *versicolor*. On the other side of the branch it is almost 100% *virginica*. The tree is not further split, even though there is a few flowers wrongly classified (4% of the validation); this is because there is no split that improves the classification and does not violate a stopping rule.

The English rules for classification of future *Iris* flowers appears as follows:

```
*----------------------------------------------------------------*
Node = 2
*----------------------------------------------------------------*
if Petal Width in mm. < 7.5
then
Tree Node Identifier = 2
Number of Observations = 34
Predicted: species=setosa = 1.00
Predicted: species=versicolor = 0.00
Predicted: species=virginica = 0.00


*----------------------------------------------------------------*
Node = 4
*----------------------------------------------------------------*
if Petal Width in mm. < 17.5 AND Petal Width in mm. >= 7.5 or
MISSING
then
Tree Node Identifier = 4
Number of Observations = 36
Predicted: species=setosa = 0.00
Predicted: species=versicolor = 0.92
Predicted: species=virginica = 0.08


*----------------------------------------------------------------*
Node = 5
*----------------------------------------------------------------*
if Petal Width in mm. >= 17.5
then
Tree Node Identifier = 5
Number of Observations = 33
Predicted: species=setosa = 0.00
Predicted: species=versicolor = 0.03
Predicted: species=virginica = 0.97
```

Misclassification rate is based on the nominal (i.e., unordered set of values, such as *Cincinnati*, *Chattanooga*, and *Spokane*) target predicted value, usually the most common value. Misclassification asks how many observations in each region (N_r observations in each region, with N_R observations in the combined region) were mispredicted (N_m), and thus is

$$M = \sum_r^R \frac{N_r}{N_R} \frac{N_m}{N_r} = \frac{1}{N_R} \sum_r^R N_m$$

Variance, used for regression trees, is similar to misclassification rate if the predicted value for the region ($\hat{t}_r$) is simply the average value of the target in that region. The variance is the usual variance formula, summed over the observations in each of the regions separately. If t_i is the target value in observation i:

$$V = \sum_r^R \frac{N_r}{N_R} \frac{1}{N_r} \sum_{i \in r} \left(t_i - \hat{t}_r\right)^2 = \frac{1}{N_R} \sum_r^R \sum_{i \in r} \left(t_i - \hat{t}_r\right)^2$$

Entropy, used with nominal targets, uses the "information" of a split. The goodness metric is then the gain of information (decrease of entropy). The entropy for a set of regions with N_t observations that have a value t for the target:

$$E = \sum_r^R \frac{N_r}{N_R} \sum_t^T \frac{N_t}{N_r} \log_2 \left(\frac{N_t}{N_r}\right)$$

Gini, also for nominal targets, is similar:

$$G = \sum_r^R \frac{N_r}{N_R} \sum_t^T \frac{N_t}{N_r} \left(1 - \frac{N_t}{N_r}\right)$$

Methods based on Chi-square, including CHAID, view the split as a two-way contingency table. For instance, Table 5.4 shows a three-region split with two target levels. Each cell in the table is the number of observations within each region with each target value. The p-value

Table 5.4 Observations

	Region A	Region B	Region C
Target value α	97	75	23
Target value β	3	50	175

of the resulting Chi-square sum determines the goodness of the split and also serves as a threshold to end growth.

The finished tree can be used to predict the value of a data set, understand how the data is partitioned, and determine variable importance. The tree structure makes it easy to see what factors were most important to determining the value of the target variable. The more important variables will be split more often and will generally be higher in the tree, where more data is being partitioned. The amount of data that a variable partitions determines how important that variable is. This importance can then be used to guide further analysis, such as regression.

Although a single decision tree is easy to understand, it can be sensitive to input data fluctuations despite the pruning process. For instance, say two variables are different only by 2 out of 1,000 observations and therefore partition the data almost identically. However, both variables do the best job of partitioning the data. Depending on how the data is used, one variable or the other may be selected, and the other will be ignored since it will likely not help partition the data much further. This is advantageous in that it means that correlated variables are compensated for automatically. However, which variable is selected as a split in the tree may change between runs based on very small changes in the data. Additionally, if the fit is not almost perfect, the later splits may be wildly different depending on which variable is chosen, resulting in considerably different trees.

Because of this, in addition to building a single decision tree, there are a number of methods that build upon using many decision trees. Random Forest™ uses bootstrap methods to create an ensemble of trees, one for each bootstrap sample. Additionally, the variables eligible to be used in splitting is randomly varied in order to decorrelate the variables. Once the forest of trees is created, they "vote" to determine the predicted value of input data. Additive methods, including AdaBoost and gradient boosting, use a number of very basic trees (often just a single split) together to predict the value. The sum of all of the trees' predictions are used to determine the final prediction, using a mapping method such as a logit function for nominal targets. Unlike forest models, the trees in additive models are created in series, in such a way as to correct mispredictions of the previous trees. This is accomplished through adjusting observation weights to make misclassified observations more important.

SUPPORT VECTOR MACHINES

I remember watching *Sesame Street* nearly every day in the morning before kindergarten. I am sure that I shouted my responses to Big Bird with as much gusto as my six-year-old body could muster. A song used often on the show titled "One of These Things" succinctly describes the purpose of support vector machines (SVMs). The song begins: "One of these things is not like the others …"

During a *Sesame Street* episode, the audience is show four items in each quadrant of the screen. Three of the items shown are the same and one is different. Usually the difference is the size or color of the item, depending on what lesson is being taught during that particular episode. This ability to differentiate items into two groups is the basic concept behind SVMs, which are especially useful when the differences are not obvious and there are hundreds or thousands of attributes to consider.

The original concept of SVMs is found in *Estimation of Dependences Based on Empirical Data* by Vapnik, in which the goal was to find optimal hyperplanes for linearly separable classes.[13] The result was that the optimal hyperplanes depended on only a small subset of the training data observations, which were called support vectors. In general, there is no one SVM algorithm; rather the term "support vector machines" refers to a general way of classifying data. Let us first look into a simple case of this original support vector machine formulation.

In Figure 5.20 we have a training data set of two groups in two dimensions: −1 (dot) and 1 (square). In general, there are many lines that can separate these two classes from each other. Two such lines are illustrated in Figure 5.21.

In addition to these two lines in Figure 5.21, you can see that there are an infinite number of lines that will separate these two groups from each other. With so many solutions that all get the correct answer, it

---

[13] A hyperplane is generalization of a two-dimensional plane (a line) that uses $n - 1$ dimensions to separate n dimensions into exactly two groups.

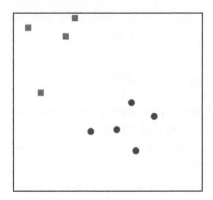

Figure 5.20 Data with Two Groups for Classification

is important to define a way to know which line is the "best" among infinite choices. Since we are interested in separating the two classes, we define the best line to be the one that maximizes the perpendicular distance from any point on either side to the line. In practice this is realized when the distance to the closest point(s) above the line is equal to the distance to the closest point(s) below the line.

You can see with the two example lines that while line A may be far away from any points in group −1, it is very close to a point in group 1. The opposite is true for line B. Neither of these lines maximizes the distance to the closest point. Let us now look at the best line (Line C) for our example in Figure 5.22.

In this case you can convince yourself visually that the line presented maximizes the distance to any point. We can add perpendicular

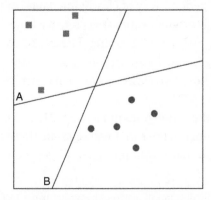

Figure 5.21 Two of Infinite Solutions to Separate into Correct Groups

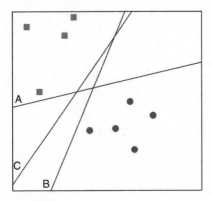

Figure 5.22 Best Separating Line

line segments representing the distance to aid in visualization. The maximization of the splitting plane provides the greatest chance to classify new observations correctly. I use a similar scheme with my children when two children want to share a treat (like a candy bar). One child determines the cut point for the candy bar, and the other gets their choice of segment. This encourages the child who is cutting the candy bar to make the two sections as even as possible. The same is true here: The algorithm is trying to find that exact equal point, normally in a high-dimensional space. (See Figure 5.23.)

The line segment from the square to the separation line has equal length to the line segment from the dot to the separation line. Finally we add two more lines, called the margin lines, to the plot. The margin line is a point of demarcation for classification. (See Figure 5.24.)

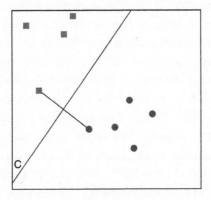

Figure 5.23 Best Separating Line with Perpendicular Reference

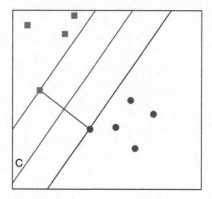

Figure 5.24 Best Separating Line with Margin Lines

As you can see, the margin lines are parallel to the separation line, and the distance from each margin line to the separation line is the same as the distance from the closest point to the separation line. Hence we call the total distance between the two margin lines the margin; often the goal of the SVM will be stated as "to maximize the margin" and make it as big as possible. Any point that lies on either margin line is considered a support vector. In our example we have only two support vectors, though in real-life applications there will likely be many support vectors. For all of you theorists, it is possible to have a problem set where every point in the data is on the margin and needed to classify points, but I have never seen this happen outside of examples designed to create this behavior.

When new data is to be classified, we look to use the separating line. A new observation is classified based on which side of the separating hyperplane it falls, so having the maximum margin will ensure minimum error in the classification of new observations. This is ultimately the question for all classification using support vector machines: Which side of the line is a new observation on? The meat of the theory for SVMs is how to make the line in a way that will minimize error on incoming data. There is also a practical consideration of taking the result of a SVM analysis and applying it to new data. The more support vectors (points on the margin) that are part of the solution, the larger the solution is to store, compute, and represent. The process is essentially to take the points on the margins, let the computer play connect-the-dots then draw a line equidistant between the two margin lines, then plot each new observation in hyperspace and evaluate into which group it belongs.

The notation for describing a support vector machine is commonly w, the normal vector to the separation line satisfies the equation: $w \times x - b = 0$ for any point x along the separation line. This b is sometimes called the bias, and it is a measure of offset of the separation line from the origin.

In the original SVM formulation, the optimal line is found by solving an optimization problem using Lagrange multipliers subject to

$$\sum\nolimits_{i=1}^{n} \alpha_i y_i = 0$$

where

alphas = Lagrange multipliers

y_i = the group (–1 or 1) of the training observation
The result is that vector w is a linear combination of the support vectors: x_i.

$$w = \sum_i \alpha_i y_i x_i$$

When we generalize the concepts from our two-dimensional example into three dimensions, separating and margin lines become separating and margin planes. In higher dimensions we refer to these as hyperplanes.

The discussion so far has assumed that the classes are linearly separable. What happens if our data looks like the plot in Figure 5.25?

As you see in Figure 5.25, there is no line that can completely separate the two classes. In 1995 in *Support-Vector Networks*, Corinna Cortes and Vladimir Vapnik addressed this case with the extension of the SVM to use a "soft margin." This formulation seeks to minimize the number of errors in the two splits and maximize the margin between these splits.

In order to solve this problem, Cortes and Vapnik introduced slack variables that measure the degree of misclassification for each data point during training. In addition, a penalty function was added to the original formulation. If a linear penalty function is used, this change results in only a slight change in the optimization in that now Lagrange multipliers are restricted by a parameter C:

$$0 \leq \alpha_i \leq C$$

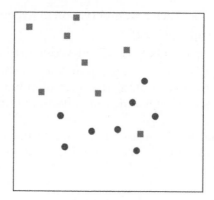

Figure 5.25 Nonlinear Class Separation

and w is still a linear combination of the support vectors x_i. If C is large, then the optimization will favor small error, while if C is small, then the optimization will favor a larger margin. It should be noted that a very small margin can lead to overfitting the data, and so while having a large C will reduce your training error, your validation error may increase.

Further work on support vector machines extended the idea of a linear separation (using a line, plane, or hyperplane) by mapping data into a higher-dimensional space. This is usually done by a method referred to as the kernel trick. It is a trick because the original data points are never explicitly calculated in the higher-dimensional space.

Where we once had the normal vector for the hyperplane satisfy $w \times x - b = 0$ for all points x on the hyperplane, we now have $k(w, x) - b = 0$ for all points x on the higher-dimensional hyperplane. Some common kernels used are:

Polynomial (nonhomogeneous): $k(x_i, x_j) = (x_i \cdot x_j + 1)^d$

Gaussian (aka radial basis function): $k(x_i, x_j) = \exp(-\gamma \| x_i - x_j \|^2)$

Sigmoid: $k(x_i, x_j) = \tanh(\kappa x_i \cdot x_j + c)$

Using other kernels can allow for correctly classifying data such as a circle of one class surrounded by another class. However, overtuning kernels has the downside of overtraining the SVM model, especially in the case of polynomial kernels. Just think about using polynomial regression to higher and higher degrees!

Some of the major drawbacks of SVMs are:

- **Binary classification.** While work has been done to extend this to multiclass, SVM models are only natively binary classifiers. This means that the algorithm can be deployed only when a binary response is needed. This makes it unsuited to interval targets such as predicting salary, age, or sales. For nominal targets, the problem will have to be recast as a binary. I used this technique while predicting a 10-level target. I created 10 SVM models, one for 1 or not 1, 2 or not 2, and so on. I then had to calculate a probability and let each model vote on the level it should be assigned. The technique works well but requires a lot of extra processing.

- **Limited interpretability.** Unlike decision trees, which are easy to interpret, or regression models, in which the coefficients have specific meaning, it is often very hard to interpret what the numbers that come out of an SVM actually mean. So using an SVM for predictive modeling requires the trade-off of predictive power with lack of interpretation.

SVM models declare a new observation as either class A or class B without providing a probability (such as 60% class A). While there are ways of mimicking this output, they do not correspond to true probabilities.

There are not widely accepted diagnostic plots to assess the quality of an SVM solution. Instead the quality of the model prediction for an independent validation set or using a K-fold cross-validation strategy is used to ensure that the model is not overfit and will generalize to new observations.

BAYESIAN METHODS NETWORK CLASSIFICATION

Thomas Bayes was a Protestant minister who lived in England in the eighteenth century. He was considered an amateur mathematician and developed his now-famous theorem while trying to prove the existence of God through the inverse probability of causes. The field of probability was very immature at this time, mostly limited to games of chance such as poker, so Bayes developed a thought experiment (the simulations of the 1700s). The experiment began with a ball randomly placed on a perfectly flat table, unseen by Bayes. Then another ball was randomly placed on the table, and an assistant would answer the question: Is the first ball to the right or left of the second ball? Successive balls would be randomly placed on the table. With more balls on the table, Bayes could visualize with increasing accuracy the position of the first ball as he was told the relative position of each new ball. Names were assigned to his method:

- "Prior" is the probability of the initial belief.
- "Likelihood" is the probability of another hypothesis given new objective data.
- "Posterior" is the probability of the newly revised belief.

Bayes's ideas have until recently been largely ignored by the statistical field.[14] While the Bayes method has some drawbacks, I firmly believe that people inherently act using Bayesian principles.

To see the Bayes theorem in action, consider the task of driving a car. Who is more likely to be involved in a car accident, a person between the ages of 16 and 24 or 25 and 69? This is not a trick question. As you probably guessed, teenagers are worse drivers and more likely to be involved in an accident. On the surface this is a confusing result; teenagers have a physical advantage with, on average, better eyesight, faster response time, and superior hearing yet the data shows that teenagers are four times more likely to be involved in a car accident than adults. Further, while teenagers make up only 10% of the population, they are involved in 12% of all fatal crashes. Not only are teenagers in more accidents, but the accidents involving teenagers tend to be more serious. One reason you might think of to explain this finding might be that teenagers are more likely to engage in risky behavior, like talking while driving or other multitasking events. This in fact is not true. In a study by State Farm Insurance, 65% of parents admit to talking on the phone while driving and only a small number of teenagers engaged in the same behavior. In another study, Ford found teenagers to be four times as distracted by phone conversations as adults. So what is the key to safe driving that

---

[14] Statisticians are generally placed in one of two groups, frequentists (the majority) and Bayesians.

teenagers with their superior physical attributes are not able to do? It is the experience and Bayesian behavior we all inherently do. As we drive, we see and observe behavior so that in the future, we are much better at predicting what will happen and we are able to focus on the relevant events of the situation. When coming to a four-way stop and seeing an oncoming car, the experienced driver will be able to instantly (perhaps instinctively) tell that the driver coming from a perpendicular street is approaching with too much speed and will not stop. As we travel along the U.S. interstate system and freeways merge, we can anticipate when cars will attempt to change lanes because we have seen this happen an untold number of times before. Teenagers do not have this knowledge base or depth of experience. Therefore, their ability to predict an outcome is limited because they do not have a well-defined prior.

In Bayesian network classification, there are several different structures each varies in how much freedom there is in drawing relationships between variables.

A Bayesian network is a graphical model that consists of two parts, G, P, where G is a directed acyclic graph (DAG) whose nodes represent random variables and arcs between nodes represent conditional dependency of the random variables and P is a set of conditional probability distributions, one for each node conditional on its parents. The conditional probability distributions for each node may be prior or learned. When building Bayesian networks from prior knowledge alone, the probabilities will be prior (Bayesian). When learning the networks from data, the probabilities will be posterior (learned).

Despite the name, Bayesian networks do not necessarily imply that they rely on Bayesian statistics. Rather, they are so called because they use Bayes' rule for probabilistic inference, as explained later. It is possible to use Bayesian statistics to learn a Bayesian network, but there are also many other techniques that are more closely related to traditional statistical methods. For example, it is common to use frequentist methods to estimate the parameters of the conditional probability distributions.

Based on the topology of the structure, there are different types of networks. Let us start with the naive Bayes network.

Naive Bayes Network

We use the data set shown in Table 5.5 as an example. It is a study of the effects of pain medication treatments on elderly patients who have chronic pain. Treatment A, treatment B, and a placebo are compared. The response variable is whether the patient reported pain or not.

The data set in Table 5.5 contains four input variables: Treatment, Sex, Age, and Duration. The variable Treatment is a nominal variable that has three levels. The gender of the patients is indicated by the nominal variable Sex. The variable Age is the age of the patients, in years, when treatment began. The duration of complaint, in months, before the treatment began is indicated by the variable Duration. For convenience, the two interval variables Age and Duration are binned into two bins, respectively.

The naive Bayes model for this data is shown in Figure 5.26. In the structure, there is a link from the target to every input variable and there are no other links. It is assumed that the input variables are independent (no interactions between variables) of each other given the target.

Table 5.5 Study of Pain Medication on the Elderly

Treatment	Sex	Age	Duration	Pain
Placebo	F	< 70	< 25	No
B	M	> = 70	< 25	No
Placebo	F	< 70	> = 25	No
Placebo	M	< 70	> = 25	Yes
B	F	< 70	> = 25	No
B	F	> = 70	< 25	No
A	F	> = 70	< 25	No
B	F	> = 70	> = 25	No
B	F	> = 70	< 25	Yes
A	M	> = 70	< 25	Yes
A	F	< 70	> = 25	No
A	F	< 70	< 25	Yes

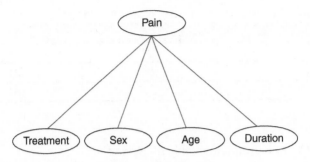

Figure 5.26 Naive Bayes Model for Pain Medication Study

Parameter Learning

Given the structure, we can learn the parameters of the conditional probability distributions, that is, $p(X_i \mid Y)$, where Y is the target (Pain), and X_i is an input variable (Treatment, Sex, Age, and Duration).

Using the maximum likelihood estimation, we can compute

$$p(X_i \mid Y) = \frac{freq(X_i, Y)}{freq(Y)}$$

where

$freq(X_i, Y)$ = frequency table of X_i and Y

$freq(Y)$ = frequency table of Y

The conditional probability distribution for Treatment is shown in Table 5.6.

We can also use a Bayesian method with Beta distribution as the prior to estimate the conditional probability distribution as

$$p(X_i \mid Y) = \frac{freq(X_i, Y) + 1}{freq(Y) + r_i}$$

Table 5.6 Conditional ML Probability Distribution for Treatments Given Target is Pain

Treatment	Pain=Yes	Pain=No
A	2/4	2/8
B	1/4	4/8
Placebo	1/4	2/8

Table 5.7 Conditional Beta Probability Distribution for Treatment

Treatment	Pain=Yes	Pain=No
A	3/7	3/11
B	2/7	5/11
Placebo	2/7	3/11

where

$freq(X_i, Y)$ = frequency table of X_i and Y

$freq(Y)$ = frequency table of Y

r_i = number of levels of X_i

The conditional probability distribution for Treatment is shown in Table 5.7.

The two estimations will be almost the same as the sample size increases. However, there is one advantage with the prior estimation: If an unseen observation has a variable with a new level, the Bayesian method can still estimate the probabilities, while the maximum likelihood estimation will estimate probability to be 0. Because the model is multiplicative, the resulting probability is 0, if any $p(X_i \mid Y) = 0$. Without the prior, $p(X_i \mid Y) = 0$ for a new level.

In the above example, we estimate the other conditional probability distributions using the prior shown in Tables 5.8, 5.9, and 5.10.

Table 5.8 Other Conditional Probability Distributions for Sex Given Target Is Pain

Sex	Pain=Yes	Pain=No
F	3/6	8/10
M	3/6	2/10

Table 5.9 Other Conditional Probability Distributions for Age Given Target Is Pain

Age	Pain=Yes	Pain=No
<70	3/6	5/10
>=70	3/6	5/10

Table 5.10 Other Conditional Probability Distributions for Duration Given Target Is Pain

Duration	Pain=Yes	Pain=No
<25	4/6	5/10
>=25	2/6	5/10

In the naive Bayes method, we can also handle interval variables directly assuming some distribution, typically Gaussian distribution. In this case, we need to estimate the parameters for the Gaussian distributions. Thanks to the independence assumption, the parameter estimation is straightforward using the maximum likelihood or Bayesian method.

This example can be extended to problems of extreme size.

Scoring

To score an observation with Treatment=A, Sex=F, Age<70, and Duration> = 25, we use the Bayes' rule as follows.

$p(Pain = Yes \mid Treatment = A, Sex = F, Age < 70, Duration \geq 25)$

$\quad = p(Pain = Yes) \times p(Treatment = A, Sex = F,$

$\qquad Age < 70, Duration \geq 25 \mid Pain = Yes) \times K$

$\quad = p(Pain = Yes) \times p(Treatment = A \mid Pain = Yes) \times$

$\qquad p(Sex = F \mid Pain = Yes) \times p(Age < 70 \mid Pain = Yes) \times$

$\qquad p(Duration \geq 25 \mid Pain = Yes) \times K$

$\quad = \dfrac{5}{14} \times \dfrac{3}{7} \times \dfrac{3}{6} \times \dfrac{3}{6} \times \dfrac{2}{6} \times K$

$\quad = 0.013 \times K$

where

$K = 1 / p(Treatment = A, Sex = F, Age < 70, Duration \geq 25)$ is a constant

Similarly we compute the conditional probability of

$p(Pain = Yes \mid Treatment = A, Sex = F, Age < 70, Duration \geq 25)$ as next.
$p(Pain = No \mid Treatment = A, Sex = F, Age < 70, Duration \geq 25)$

$\quad = p(Pain = No) \times p(Treatment = A, Sex = F, Age$

$\qquad < 70, Duration \geq 25 \mid Pain = Yes) \times K$

$\quad = p(Pain = No) \times p(Treatment = A \mid Pain = No) \times$

$\qquad p(Sex = F \mid Pain = No) \times p(Age < 70 \mid Pain = No) \times$

$\qquad p(Duration \geq 25 \mid Pain = No) \times K$

$\quad = \dfrac{9}{14} \times \dfrac{3}{11} \times \dfrac{8}{10} \times \dfrac{5}{10} \times \dfrac{5}{10} \times K$

$\quad = 0.035 \times K$

Since

$$p(Pain = No \mid Treatment = A, Sex = F, Age < 70, Duration >= 25) >$$
$$p(Pain = Yes \mid Treatment = A, Sex = F, Age < 70, Duration >= 25),$$

we will score this observation as *Pain = No*.

Learning a Bayesian Network

Bayesian networks can be used for both supervised learning and unsupervised learning. In unsupervised learning, there is no target variable; therefore, the only network structure is DAG. In supervised learning, we need only the variables that are around the target, that is, the parents, the children, and the other parents of the children (spouses). Besides the naive Bayes, there are other types of network structures: tree-augmented naive Bayes (TAN), Bayesian network-augmented naive Bayes (BAN), parent child Bayesian network (PC), and Markov blanket Bayesian network (MB).

These network structures differ in which links are allowed between nodes. We classify them based on the three types of links (from target to input, from input to target, and between the input nodes) and whether to allow spouses of the target. The summary is shown in Table 5.11. Notice that TAN and BAN both allow links from the target to the input and between the input nodes. However, TAN has a tree structure among the input nodes, while BAN allows a Bayesian network (DAG) structure among the input nodes.

To learn these networks, we need not only to determine the parameters of the conditional probability distributions but also to learn the network structures. For TAN, one approach is to find the maximum

Table 5.11 Allowed Links between Nodes by Network Type

Network	Target -> Input	Input -> Target	Input -> Input	Spouse
Naive	Yes	No	No	No
TAN	Yes	No	Yes	No
BAN	Yes	No	Yes	No
PC	Yes	Yes	Yes	No
MB	Yes	Yes	Yes	Yes

spanning tree[15] among the input nodes, while the weight of an edge is the mutual information of the two nodes. For BAN, PC, or MB, a greedy approach is typically used to find a local optimum, because the number of possible structures is superexponential to the number of nodes in the network.

In general, there are two approaches to learning the network structure: one is score based, and the other is constraint based. The score-based approach uses a score function to measure how well a structure fits the training data and tries to find the structure that has the best score. The constraint-based approach uses independence tests to determine the edges and the directions.

In the house alarm[16] example shown in Figure 5.27, there are five variables: an Earthquake has occurred, a Burglary has occurred, an Alarm has sounded, John Calls and Mary Calls the authorities, each representing an event. For short, they are denoted as E, B, A, J, and M respectively. All variables are binary, with T meaning the presence of the event and F the absence of the event.

We see that the Alarm sounds for one of two reasons: either an Earthquake or a Burglary. As a result of an Alarm, the two neighbors, John and Mary, may call the owner of the house that has the Alarm. This is a parent child network structure, if Alarm is the target. The two causes of the Alarm, Earthquake or Burglary, are the parents, and John calling the authorities or Mary calling the authorities are the children to alarm.

The conditional probability distribution for each node is shown beside the node. For example, the probability of Earthquake is 0.02 and Burglary is 0.01. Suppose both Earthquake and Burglary happen, the probability of the Alarm is 0.95. If none of them happen (a false alarm), the Alarm will go off with probability of 0.001. If the Alarm

---

[15] A spanning tree is a tree that connects all nodes in the network. A maximum spanning tree is a spanning tree that has the maximum total weight of the edges among all possible spanning trees in the network. The weight of an edge is the mutual information of the two connecting nodes.

[16] Judea Pearl in, *Probabilistic Reasoning in Intelligent Systems: Networks of Plausible Inference*, published a very famous example using a fire alarm. This is an adaptation of that example.

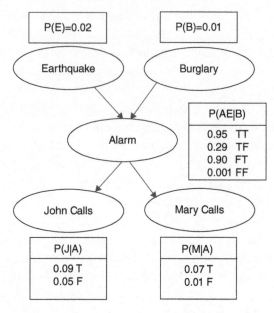

Figure 5.27 House Alarm Example

goes off, John calls with probability of 0.90 and Mary calls with probability of 0.70 respectively.

The network structure together with the conditional probability distributions completely determine the Bayesian network model, that is, the joint probability distribution of the variables is factored to the product of the conditional probability distributions. More formally, let U be the set of variables, X is a variable in U, $pa(X)$ is the set of parents of X, then $p(U) = \prod (X \mid pa(X))$.

Inference in Bayesian Networks

Once we have a Bayesian network (from a prior or learned from data), we can infer the probabilities of interest from the model. For example, in the house alarm problem, we want to determine the probability of the Alarm sounding given observations of the other variables. Suppose we observe that there is a Burglary to the house but no Earthquake, and Mary calls but John does not; what is the probability that the Alarm sounds? We can compute the probability as follows.

$$P(A \mid B = T, E = F, M = T, J = F) = \frac{P(A = T, B = T, E = F, M = T, J = F)}{P(B = T, E = F, M = T, J = F)}$$

Using the factorization of the conditional probability distributions, we compute the join distribution as follows.

$$P(A = T, B = T, E = F, M = T, J = F) = P(B = T) \times P(E = F)*$$

$$P(A = T \mid B = T, E = F) \times P(M = T \mid A = T) \times P(J = F \mid A = T)$$

$$= 0.01 \times 0.98 \times 0.94 \times 0.70 \times 0.1$$

$$= 0.000645$$

$$P(B = T, E = F, M = T, J = F) = P(A = T, B = T, E = F, M = T, J = F) +$$

$$P(A = F, B = T, E = F, M = T, J = F)$$

$$= 0.000645 + P(B = T) \times P(E = F) \times$$

$$P(A = F \mid B = T, E = F) \times P(M = T \mid A = F) \times P(J = F \mid A = F)$$

$$= 0.000645 + 0.01 \times 0.98 \times 0.06 \times 0.01 \times 0.95$$

$$= 0.000645 + 0.000006$$

$$= 0.000651$$

Finally, we have

$$P(A \mid B = T, E = F, M = T, J = F) = \frac{0.000645}{0.000651}$$

$$= 0.99$$

Scoring for Supervised Learning

Given a Bayesian network $< G, P >$, let $X = (X1, X2, \ldots, Xn)$ be the set of variables and $Y = Xn$ be the target variable. We can score an observation $(x_1, x_2, \ldots, x_{n-1})$ as the level with the maximum probability given the observed input values.

$$\text{argmax}_c p(T = c \mid x1, x2, \ldots, xn - 1) = \frac{P(x_1, x_2, \ldots, x_{n-1}, c)}{p(x_1, x_2, \ldots, x_{n-1})}$$

$$= \frac{\prod_i p(x_i \mid pa(X_i))}{p(x_1, x_2, \ldots, x_{n-1})}$$

where

c = a level of the target

$pa(X_i)$ = the set of parents of X_i

Since the denominator is constant for all levels of the target, it is sufficient to calculate the numerator.

In the house alarm example, given that there is a Burglary to the house but no Earthquake, and Mary calls but John does not, what do we predict for the Alarm? We can compute the probabilities of the two levels (T and F) of Alarm.

$$P(A = T, B = T, E = F, M = T, J = F) = 0.000645$$

$$P(A = F, B = T, E = F, M = T, J = F) = 0.000006$$

Since

$P(A = T, B = T, E = F, M = T, J = F) > P(A = F, B = T, E = F, M = T, J = F),$
we predict that the Alarm will go off.

Bayesian network classification is a very effective technique for predictive modeling and also for variable selection. Many software packages have implementations of these different structures. One key measure to evaluation of different packages is the parallelism and ability to deal with wide data. From my experience, Bayesian network classifiers can perform well on data that is hundreds of thousands of columns and, depending on the implementation, can even work on dense data.

ENSEMBLE METHODS

An ensemble model is the combination of two or more models. Ensembles can be combined in several ways. A common and my personal preference is a voting strategy, where each model votes on the classification of an observation and then in a democratic fashion the classification with the most votes win. Another strategy is to average the predictions from the different methods to make a numeric prediction.

Boosting and bagging are accumulation model techniques that resample the training data to create new models for each sample that is drawn.

Bagging is the most straightforward of ensemble methods. Simply stated, it takes repeated unweighted samples from the data. Each observation can be included in a sample only once (without replacement within a sample), but observations are eligible to be included in all samples (sampling with replacement across samples). With bagging, it is possible that an observation is included in each sample or an observation is included in none. Under normal conditions, neither of these cases is likely. Because the samples are unweighted, no weight is given to misclassified observations from previous samples. To implement a bagging strategy, you decide how many samples to generate and how large each sample should be. There is a trade-off in these two values. If you take a small percentage of the observations, you will need to take a larger number of samples. I usually take about a 30% sample and take seven samples so that each observation is likely to be selected into a couple of samples. After the samples have been taken and a model fit, those models are then accumulated to provide the final model. This final model is generally more stable than the single model using all the data. Bagging is particularly effective when the underlying model is a decision tree. I have not found benefit to bagging regression or neural network models.

Why does bagging work? In the case of the decision tree model, by taking a sample of the data, you will likely find different splits and a different-looking tree for each sample. None of these tree models is as good as the tree fit on all the data, but when the weaker models are combined, their predictive power is often better than the single model built on the full data. This is because excluding some observations allows weaker relationships to be exploited.

Boosting is very similar to bagging but with the major difference that in boosting, reweighting occurs after each sample model is fit to "boost" the performance of the weak model built on the sampled data. The weights of the misclassified observations are increased so that they are more likely to be selected and therefore be exploited by a subtle relationship in the data. This normally has an improved effect on the overall model when comparing boosting results with bagging results. The trade-off is that boosting must be done in a sequential manner because of the reweighting while bagging can be done in parallel, assuming you have sufficient system resources. In my personal experience, I tend to use boosting for classification models and bagging for interval prediction models

Random forest is an ensemble tree technique that builds a large number of trees that are weak classifiers and then are used to vote in some manner to build a stable and strong classifier that is better than the average tree created in the forest. This falls under the axiom that the whole is greater than the sum of its parts. One of the fundamental ideas in random forest is that a subset of the observations and a subset of the variables are taken. This sampling in both dimensions ensures that all variables are considered, not just the dominant few as is usually seen in decision trees. What is the right number of variables to consider in each tree? A good rule of thumb is to use is the square root of the number of candidate variables.

There are a number of tuning parameters to be considered in the training of a random forest model. Here are the high-level dimensions and my recommendations for defaults, given my experience in modeling. Specific problems might require deviations from these recommendations, but I have found success across many industries and problem types.

- Number of trees
- Variables to try
- Number of splits to consider
- Number of observations in each tree

CHAPTER **6**

Segmentation

Segmentation is a collection of methods used to divide items, usually people or products, into logical mutually exclusive groups called segments. These segmentation methods include several functions for identifying the best variables to be used in defining the groups, the variables to be used in analyzing these groups, assigning observations to the clusters, analyzing/validating these clusters, and profiling them to see the common characteristics of the groups.

A well-defined segment has the following features:

- It is homogeneous with respect to a similarity measure within itself.
- It is distinct from other segments with respect to that similarity measure.

Rummikub is a tile-based game for two to four players that was invented by Ephraim Hertzano.[1] Hertzano was born in Romania and developed the game when card games were outlawed under

---

The data analysis for this chapter was generated using SAS Enterprise Miner software, Version 13.1 of the SAS System for Windows. Copyright © 2013 SAS Institute Inc. SAS and all other SAS Institute Inc. product or service names are registered trademarks or trademarks of SAS Institute Inc., Cary, NC, USA.

[1] Rummikub won the Spiel des Jahres (Germany's Game of the Year) in 1980.

communist rule. The game consists of 104 numbered tiles plus two jokers. The tiles are divided into four unique color groups (usually red, blue, green, and orange) and numbered 1 to 13 so that there are two tiles for each number color combination. The game begins by each player drawing tiles from the 106 facedown tiles—I do not know the official number you are supposed to draw but in my family we draw 20.

After the tiles are drawn, each player organizes their tiles without revealing them to the other players. Once players have had a chance to organize their tiles, play begins. Dean house rules require the oldest player to go first. During a player's first turn, they must create valid sets exclusively from their tiles. A set is either a run of at least three consecutive tiles of the same color or at least three unique colored tiles with the same number. For example, tiles 4, 5, and 6 in blue is a valid run and three 11 tiles, one red, blue, and orange, is a valid set, as shown in Figure 6.1. The official rules require that the initial meld must have a certain value of the summed numbers played. The initial meld threshold was 50 before 1988, then it was dropped to 30; in my

Figure 6.1 Example of Valid Sets in Rummikub

family, kids under 5 do not have an initial threshold until they have beaten their father. If a player cannot meet the initial meld threshold, then they draw a tile and the play passes to the next younger player. After a player has completed the initial meld (hopefully on the first turn), then play continues with players laying down valid sets or runs from their tiles or reorganizing the existing tiles to place their tiles. The objective of the game is to place all of your tiles. The first person to do so is declared the winner. The jokers can be used at any time in place of any numbered tile.

The game of Rummikub is a hands-on experience in segmentation. The tiles can be part of only one group of tiles (either a set or a run) at any particular time, just as segmentations must create mutually exclusive groups. The strategy for partitioning the tiles is different among different players. Each player in my family has a slightly different system for organizing their tiles and how they choose to play their titles through the game.

In segmentation for business or Rummikub, there is not a single "right" answer, and the best segmentation strategy can change through the course of the game just as segmentation strategies in organizations must adapt to changing market conditions to be successful. I often have three segments to my tiles initially. I have tiles lower than 5 for making sets, tiles higher than 9 for making sets, and tiles between 5 and 9 for making runs. I always hope for an additional segment of jokers, which I keep separate until I can use them to place all of my remaining tiles and win the game. I have these three segments because of the challenges of forming runs. In order to create a run with a black 1 tile, I must have the black 2 and black 3 tiles; at the beginning of the game, I have only a 3.7% (4/106 because there are two tiles for each color) chance of getting that combination. In contrast, to get a set of 1 tiles, I have a 5.6% chance (6/106 because there are eight tiles for each number, but a set cannot contain two tiles of the same color so that leaves two tiles for 1 orange, 1 red, and 1 blue). The same probability situation occurs at the upper extreme of the numbers. The middle numbers segment has better odds for runs because there are multiple numbers that can be drawn or used from the existing board to create those runs. In the case of an 8 red, I can use 6 red, 7 red, 9 red, or 10 red to create a run.

My youngest son, who has just started playing Rummikub, has a simpler strategy with just two segments, jokers and everything else. He is much stronger at putting runs together than sets so runs dominate his play. (I think this is due to the challenge of not having the same color in a set, which he sometimes forgets and his older siblings are quick to point out). This highlights another parallel between segmentation in the game and business: For most applications, a simple segmentation strategy is better than no strategy at all. If my youngest son were to have just one segment (all tiles played equally), the joker would be played very early in the game and provide him little advantage to the point of being essentially wasted.

The segmentation of the jokers from the numbered tiles points out the difference between clustering and segmentation. The terms are often used interchangeably because they are so closely related, but segmentation is a superset of clustering. Clustering is done by an algorithmic method, and it is mechanical. Segmentation often uses clustering techniques and then applies business rules like the treatment of keeping jokers in a special segment until the end of the game.

Many companies build their own segments but others prefer to buy them to aid primarily in their marketing activities. One commercial set of segments is done by PRIZM (which is currently owned by Nielsen). When I was considering moving from northern Virginia to Cary, North Carolina, I spent hours reading the descriptions of the different segments and imagining the people who lived there. PRIZM uses 66 segments to describe the people across America. Here is an example of three segments to give you an idea of the type of description and characterization given:

19 Home Sweet Home

Widely scattered across the nation's suburbs, the residents of Home Sweet Home tend to be upper-middle-class married couples living in mid-sized homes with few children. The adults in the segment, mostly between the ages of 25 and 54, have gone to college and hold

professional and white-collar jobs. With
their upscale incomes and small families,
these folks have fashioned comfortable
lifestyles, filling their homes with toys, TV
sets and pets.

07 Money & Brains

The residents of Money & Brains seem to
have it all: high incomes, advanced degrees
and sophisticated tastes to match their
credentials. Many of these city dwellers,
predominantly white with a high
concentration of Asian Americans, are
married couples with few children who live
in fashionable homes on small, manicured
lots.

51 Shotguns & Pickups

The segment known as Shotguns & Pickups
came by its moniker honestly: It scores near
the top of all lifestyles for owning hunting
rifles and pickup trucks. These Americans
tend to be young, working-class couples
with large families—more than half have two
or more kids—living in small homes and
manufactured housing. Nearly a third of
residents live in mobile homes, more than
anywhere else in the nation.

These segments are designed to be informative yet concise and
allow organizations to match the goods or services with those people
most likely to respond positively. For certain specialized applications,
each segment may have additional constraints that would need to be
satisfied as well.

Since each segment is homogeneous, which means lower variance
within the individual segments, it is possible to get better predictive
models for each segment than you could achieve by building a predictive model for the entire population. Plainly stated, segmentation will
often improve your ability to make correct predictions or classifica-
tions during predictive modeling activities, assuming each segment is
large enough to build quality predictive models.

Feature films are another example of segmentation. Movies are classified into categories for many reasons. Perhaps the most important is that if they were not, the list of film choices would overwhelm most people and be too difficult to navigate effectively. We segment movies by their genre—horror, sci-fi, action, romantic comedy, and so on. Movies are also segmented by their rating and several other categories. I doubt there is a movie that appeals to the entire population, so production studios and sponsors want to understand the specific demographic for which this film is intended. Fast food chains would never want to distribute action figures from an R-rated horror film with their children's menu. Likewise, PG-rated animation films of a classic Grimm fairy tale would not be expected to be popular in the 21- to 25-year-old male demographic.

CLUSTER ANALYSIS

Clustering is the process of organizing objects into self-similar groups by discovering the boundaries between these groups algorithmically using a number of different statistical algorithms and methods. Cluster analysis does not make any distinction between dependent and independent variables. It examines the entire set of interdependent relationships to discover the similarity relationships between the objects in order to identify the clusters. Cluster analysis can also be utilized as a dimension reduction method in which the number of objects are grouped into a set of clusters, and then a reduced set of variables are used for predictive modeling. This practice helps reduce issues related to multicollinearity.

Clustering can be grouped into three categories, unsupervised, semisupervised, and supervised:

1. **Unsupervised clustering.** The objective of unsupervised clustering is to maximize the intracluster similarity and to minimize the intercluster similarity, given a similarity/dissimilarity measure. It uses a specific objective function (e.g., a function that minimizes the intraclass distances to find tight clusters). It uses a data set that has no target variable. K-means and hierarchical clustering are the most widely used unsupervised clustering techniques in segmentation.

2. **Semisupervised clustering.** In addition to the similarity measure that is also used in unsupervised clustering, semisupervised clustering utilizes other guiding/adjusting domain information to improve the clustering results. This domain information can be pairwise constraints (must-link or cannot-link) between the observations or target variables for some of the observations. This guiding information is used either for adjusting the similarity measure or for modifying the search for clusters in order to bias the search. In addition to the objectives for unsupervised clustering, semisupervised clustering has the objective of obtaining high consistency between the clusters and the guiding/adjusting domain information.

3. **Supervised clustering.** The goal of supervised clustering is to identify clusters that have high probability densities with respect to individual classes (class-uniform clusters). It is used when there is a target variable and a training set that includes the variables to cluster.

DISTANCE MEASURES (METRICS)

An objective way to evaluate segments is based on a similarity or dissimilarity between the objects and clusters in the data set. Many possible distance measures can be used to compute clusters. The most common are mentioned below. Two types of distance can be measured and accessed: the distance between objects and the distance between clusters. Both are important metrics depending on the clustering application.

1. **Distance measures between objects**

   They are used to measure the distances between the objects in the data set that is used for clustering.

   - **Euclidean distance.** It is basically the geometric distance between objects in the multidimensional space. It corresponds to the length of the shortest path between two objects. It is used to obtain sphere-shaped clusters.

   - **City block (Manhattan) distance**. It corresponds to the sum of distances along each dimension and is less sensitive to outliers. It is used to obtain diamond-shaped clusters.

- **Cosine similarity measure.** It is calculated by measuring the cosine of angle between two objects. It is used mostly to compute the similarity between two sets of transaction data.

2. **Distance measures between clusters**

    They are used to measure the distances between clusters. The measures that are used in hierarchical clustering are:

- **Average linkage.** It is the average distance between all the points in two clusters.

- **Single linkage.** It is the distance between nearest points in two clusters

- **Complete linkage.** It is the distance between farthest points in two clusters.

EVALUATING CLUSTERING

Since clustering is used mostly in an unsupervised way, there needs to be a measure to evaluate the quality of the clusters provided from a particular algorithm. These evaluation criteria are used mainly to find out the variability or noise in clusters, to find the optimal number of clusters for the data, to compare the clustering algorithms on the quality of their solutions, and to compare two sets of results obtained from cluster analysis.

1. **Internal evaluation criterion.** It is part of cluster analysis and is specific to the method. It is computed for the data that is used for cluster analysis. Though the objective functions for all the clustering algorithms are very similar (high intracluster similarity and low intercluster similarity), the evaluation criteria that are used in different algorithms differ one from another. For example, while sum of squares error (SSE) can be used for evaluating the k-means clustering algorithm, it cannot be used for density-based clustering algorithms.

2. **External evaluation criterion.** This criterion can be obtained using a separate data set that was not used for cluster analysis. It is used to measure how representative the clusters are with respect to a true cluster when the class labels are given or how consistent they are with respect to different clusters

when they are obtained using different parameters/methods. It can be measured in terms of purity, entropy, random index, or F-measure.

NUMBER OF CLUSTERS

For some of the unsupervised clustering algorithms, such as k-means, one of the main questions is "How many clusters are in the data?" or asked another way "What is the right number of clusters to segment my data?" There are several objective metrics such as gap and cubic clustering criteria (CCC). CCC uses a simulated reference distribution to evaluate the right number of clusters. In my work at SAS, we have recently filed a patent that extends on the CCC method by generating many reference distributions that are aligned with principal components. This method is called aligned box criteria (ABC), and it has the advantage of being more straightforward in the diagnostic interpretation.

Why was ABC not developed until now? As was discussed in Part One of this book, the computational power that has recently become commodity is a major factor. Instead of generating just one reference distribution, you can do principal component analysis for each number of clusters to be considered and generate reference distributions based on these values with hundreds to thousands of variables considered in modern segmentation problems. This is infeasible without significant computational resources.

Here is an example of unsupervised segmentation using clustering. I have generated an X and Y variable from seven different distributions. Each distribution has 1,000 points. The data is plotted in Figure 6.2 with each distribution getting its own symbol.

Without the symbols, it would be a very difficult problem for a human to segment all of these points into seven different classes. To assist pract itioners a grid search method can be used. Cluster analysis is performed multiple times with a different number of clusters each time and the results are then analyzed to figure out the best choices for the number of clusters in the data. Using the ABC method, we get the diagnostic plot shown in Figure 6.3 indicating the possible candidates for the true number of clusters. This objective measure gives a starting point to determine the "right" number of segmentations for your problem.

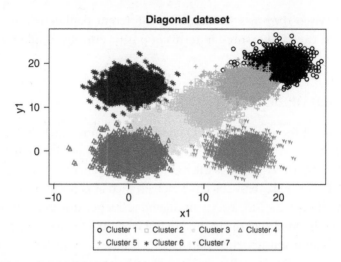

Figure 6.2 Plot of Seven Different Sets of Generated Data

How this plot is interpreted is as follows: Beginning with the minimum number of clusters, we see a decrease in the Y value. After Y starts to increase, we search for the peak values according to the Y

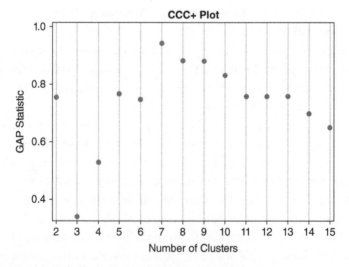

Figure 6.3 Diagnostic Plot to Assess the Best Number of Clusters

values. For example, here we see that the first peak value of Y is at 5 number of clusters and the global peak of Y is at 7 number of the clusters. Both 5 and 7 are good candidates for this cluster set. The algorithm found 3 clusters in the diagonal region of the data set for 5 number of clusters, while it found 5 clusters in the same region for 7 number of clusters.

K-MEANS ALGORITHM

K-means is one of the most widely used clustering techniques because of its simplicity and speed. It partitions the data into k clusters by assigning each object to its closest cluster centroid (the mean value of the variables for all objects in that particular cluster) based on the distance measure used. It is more robust to different types of variables. In addition, it is fast for large data sets, which are common in segmentation.

The basic algorithm for *k*-means works as follows:

1. Choose the number of clusters, k.
2. Select k cluster centroids (e.g., randomly chosen k objects from the data set).
3. Assign each object to the nearest cluster centroid.
4. Recompute the new cluster centroid.
5. Repeat step 3 and 4 until the convergence criterion is met (e.g., the assignment of objects to clusters no longer changes over multiple iterations) or maximum iteration is reached.

Many issues need to be considered in *k*-means clustering:

- The *k*-means algorithm requires the number of clusters k as an input. The ABC method can be used to estimate the number of clusters.
- The similarity/distance measure should be selected depending on the task.
- Clusters may converge to a local minimum. Due to this issue, the clusters that are obtained might not be the right ones. To avoid this, it might be helpful to run the algorithm with different initial cluster centroids and compare the results.

The k-means algorithm can take advantage of data parallelism. When the data objects are distributed to each processor, step 3 can be parallelized easily by doing the assignment of each object into the nearest cluster in parallel. In order to update cluster centroids at each node for every iteration, communication of cluster centroid–related information between nodes can also be added in steps 2 and 4.

HIERARCHICAL CLUSTERING

Hierarchical clustering generates clusters that are organized into a hierarchical structure. Visualizing this hierarchical structure can be used to understand the structure of clusters in the data set in addition to the clusters themselves. This technique only requires a measure of similarity between objects. It does not require you to specify the number of clusters. You can obtain any number of clusters by cutting the hierarchical structure at a proper level. There are two main categories for hierarchical clustering:

1. **Divisive clustering.** This is a top-down approach. It considers all objects in a big, single cluster first and then divides the clusters into smaller groups at each level.
2. **Agglomerative clustering.** This is a bottom-up approach. It considers each object to be an individual cluster first, and then it combines them into bigger clusters at each level according to their similarity. Clusters can be generated by minimizing the squared Euclidean distance to the center mean (Ward's method) or based on the distance between clusters (single linkage, complete linkage, average linkage methods).

PROFILING CLUSTERS

Once clusters are computed using one of the clustering techniques, an analysis should be done in order to describe each cluster. This is called profiling. This analysis can be done in terms of the internal variables that are used in the cluster analysis and the external variables that are important for the analysis of the segments. For example, you can do cluster analysis using the age and income of the customers as internal variables. After you obtained the clusters, you can do an analysis on the demographic information of customers for each cluster. Mean, range, or standard deviation of variables in each cluster is commonly used in profiling.

CHAPTER 7

Incremental Response Modeling

A standard part of marketing campaigns in many industries is to offer coupons to encourage adoption of the new goods or service. This enticement is often essential for success because it provides some additional incentive to persuade customers to switch products if they are currently satisfied with the goods or service in question. For example, if I am a longtime buyer of laundry detergent XYZ, to get me to try a competitor's laundry product detergent ABC, I will need some incentive great enough to get to move outside my comfort zone of buying detergent XYZ on my trips to the store. This incentive or inducement could be superior performance, but I will never know that the performance is superior unless I try the product. Another inducement could be value. Detergent ABC cleans just as well as detergent XYZ, and I get a larger quantity of detergent ABC for the same price as detergent XYZ. This strategy, like superior quality, is also predicated in me trying the product. All strategies that will successfully convert from detergent XYZ to detergent ABC require me to try the product, and the most common way to do that is to give me a coupon. Coupons are very common for most household products and packaged foods. These coupons can, in some cases, be successful in changing buying behavior from one product to another product. Now consider this alternative case: I have been buying detergent XYZ regularly, but I am not very happy with it and I have decided to switch to detergent ABC because of a new ad I saw while watching TV. Now when I receive a coupon for detergent ABC that I had planned to buy anyway, I purchase my detergent ABC, but the manufacturer yields less profit because I purchased a product I had already planned to at a lower price than I was already willing to pay.

This is what incremental response modeling methods do: determine those people who purchased the product because of an inducement (coupon) in order to maximize the profit for the organization.

BUILDING THE RESPONSE MODEL

The results of a marketing campaign will fall into one of three groups: people who will not purchase the product regardless of the incentive, those who switched products because of the campaign, and those who were going to switch already and can now purchase the product at a reduced rate. Of these three groups, we would like to target with our marketing only those who switched just because of the coupon. There is a fourth category that I will discuss here and not refer to again. This is the group referred to as sleeping dogs; they are mostly encountered in political campaigns, not marketing campaigns. Sleeping dogs are those people who purchase your product or subscribe to your political view but by including them in a campaign they respond negatively and leave your brand.

Public radio is another example to demonstrate incremental response. Public radio, supported by listeners, has fund drives several times throughout the year to raise money to support the programming. Many listeners donate as soon as they hear the fund drive begin because they want to support the programming and feel a duty to do so. Another group probably would not donate to the station except for the appeal of a coffee mug, tote, video collection, or some other gift to reward them for their generosity that sways them to pick up the phone or go to the website and contribute. The problem for public broadcasting is it cannot discern between the two groups. If it could

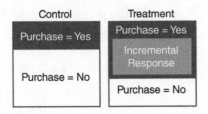

Figure 7.1 Control versus Treatment

discern between the groups, it could save the costs associated with those giveaway items and therefore reduce overall cost.

The method behind incremental response modeling is this: Begin with a treatment and control group. These groups should follow a methodology from the clinical trial literature. The treatment is a coupon. Note that you can use multiple treatments, but here we will discuss only the binary case.

Once you have divided your sample into the two assigned groups, administered either the treatment or the control, and then gathered the results, you can begin to apply this methodology. Figure 7.1 shows the difference between the control group and treatment group. The treatment group received the coupon for detergent ABC while the control group received no coupon. You can see that the coupon was effective in increasing sales (based on the size of the box labeled "Purchase=Yes"), but the top section in the treatment group represents all people who purchased the detergent. The ones in the box labeled "Incremental Response" purchased because of the coupon and the rest would have purchased regardless. Therefore, the treatment group did not maximize profit because the detergent was sold at a lower price than could have otherwise been demanded. It is rare but possible that in some cases the treatment group, those who received the coupon, could actually generate less profit than the control group, doing nothing.

MEASURING THE INCREMENTAL RESPONSE

A traditional approach to accessing the incremental response is using a differencing technique from two predictive models. Take the likelihood to purchase from the predictive model built for the treatment group:

$$P_t(y = 1 \mid x)$$

The likelihood to purchase for the control group is similar:

$$P_c(y = 1 \mid x)$$

The incremental response likelihood can be calculated as the difference

$$P_D = P_t(y = 1 \mid x) - P_t(y = 1 \mid x)$$

Then sort the resulting P_D from largest to smallest, and the top deciles are the incremental responders. Any predictive model can be employed in the differencing technique, such as the regression-based differencing model and the tree-based differencing model.

An improved method is to look only at the control group, the people who did not get the coupon, and classify each person as an outlier or not. Several techniques can be used for classifying outliers when you have only one group. A method that has good results classifying outliers is one-class support vector machines (SVMs).

Recently a new method was suggested that uses an outlier detection technique, particularly the one-class SVM. The suggested method uses the control group data to train the model and uses the treatment group as a validation set. The detected outliers are considered as incremental responses. This new method shows much better results than the differencing technique. The technique is illustrated with plots below, but more details can be found in the paper by Lee listed in the references.

In Figure 7.2, we see a graphical representation of the points from the control group that have been identified as outliers. The dots closer to the origin than the dashed line are classified as part of the negative class, and other dots up and to the right of the dashed line are classified to the positive class. The points in the negative class are considered outliers (those between the origin and the dashed line). They receive this designation because there are particular features, or a combination of many features, that identify them as different from the overall group.

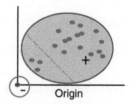

Figure 7.2 Outlier Identification of Control Group

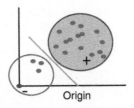

Origin

Figure 7.3 Separation of Responders and Nonresponders in the Control Group

One reason to identify some of the points in the control group as outliers is to narrow the region that the control group identifies so that we can better determine which observations are incremental responders when we apply the model to the treatment group. To apply this to our example, we would look at the people who purchased detergent ABC and then, using a one-class SVM model, identify some of those as outliers. This would leave us a set of ranges for each attribute of our customers that we can use to identify them as people who would purchase detergent ABC without a coupon, as shown in Figure 7.3.

The region of the responders for the control group as shown by the larger circle in Figure 7.3 this region can then be projected to the treatment group. Applying this region to the treatment group will identify the incremental responders, those individuals who purchased detergent ABC because of the coupon. This is illustrated graphically in Figure 7.4. This is only a representation in two dimensions. In practice, this would be in dozens, hundreds, or even thousands of dimensions.

Figure 7.4 shows the projection of the control group, those who bought detergent ABC without a coupon after the outliers were removed using a one-class SVM model and projecting the region to the treatment group, those who bought detergent ABC after being sent a coupon. To interpret this plot, examine the different parts. The first group to identify is the treatment group that falls inside the oval; these are responders who were unaffected by the coupon. This means that for those people inside the upper oval, the coupon did not influence their purchasing choice (buy detergent ABC regardless of the promotion either to buy detergent ABC or to not buy). The data points outside of the oval in the treatment response group

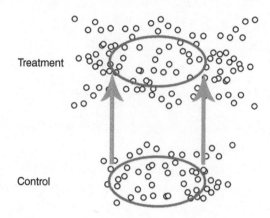

Figure 7.4 Projection of Control Group to Treatment Group

are the potential incremental responders. Those are the people who purchased because of the treatment; in this specific example, the coupon for detergent ABC. I used the word "potential" above because there is no definitive way in real life to objectively measure those people who responded only as a result of the treatment. This can be tested empirically using simulation, and that work has illustrated the effectiveness of this method. Figure 7.5 is an example of a simulation study.

Figure 7.5 shows 1,300 responders to the treatment group. This includes 300 true incremental responders. The method described above identified 296 observations as incremental responders, and 280 of

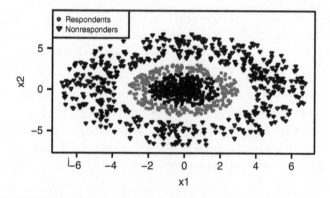

Figure 7.5 Simulation of 1,300 Responders to Coupon Offer

Table 7.1 Classification of Incremental Responders

	Correctly Classified	Falsely Classified
Responders	280	20
Nonresponders	986	16

those identified were true positives. This is all the more impressive because, as you can see, there is no simple way to use straight lines and separate the gray true incremental responders from the black nonincremental responders. This leaves 20 true responders who were not identified and 16 who were incorrectly identified. See Table 7.1 for a tabular view.

This simulation yields a 5.4% error rate, which is a significant improvement over the differencing method explained at the beginning of the chapter. Incremental response modeling holds much promise in the areas of targeted advertising and microsegmentation. The ability to select only those people who will respond only when they receive the treatment is very powerful and can contribute significantly to increased revenue. Consider the typical coupon sells the goods or service at 90% of the regular price (a 10% discount). Every correctly identified true incremental responder will raise revenue 0.9 and every correctly identified nonincremental responder (those who are not influenced by the treatment either to purchase or not) will raise revenue by 0.1 because those items will not be sold at a discount needlessly. Then add in the nominal cost of the treatment—ad campaign, postage, printing costs, channel management. We have the following revenue adjustments:

$$Incremental\ Revenue = 0.9r + 0.1n - campaign\ costs$$

where
r = incremental responders who will purchase the product if they receive the coupon but otherwise will not
n = nonresponders who will not buy the product even if they received the coupon
By taking the simulation example but increasing the error rate to nearly double at 10%, you can see the advantage of using incremental response:

Incremental response revenue $= 333$ *units* $= .9(270) + .1(900) -$ *fixed costs*

compared to:

Control only $= 100$ *units* $= .9(0) + .1(1000) -$ *campaign costs*

Treatment only $= 270$ *units* $= .9(300) + .1(0) -$ *campaign costs*

for the control and treatment-only groups. When looking at the fixed costs of each scenario, the treatment will have the largest effect because a coupon is being sent to each of the 1,300 people. This will be followed by the incremental response group, where coupons are sent only to those predicted to respond; and finally the control group, where there are no campaign costs because of the lack of campaign.

Treatment campaign costs > Incremental reponse campaign costs >
Control campaign costs = 0

When the campaign costs are added to the calculations, the incremental response is an even better option to either the treatment or the control group. This increasing amount of information that is made available will over time reduces the error rates, yielding even larger revenues for those organizations that leverage this powerful technique.

CHAPTER **8**

Time Series Data Mining

Times series data mining is an emerging field that holds great opport unities for conversion of data into information. It is intuitively obvious to us that the world is filled with time series data—actually transactional data—such as point-of-sales (POS) data, financial (stock market) data, and Web site data. Transactional data is time-stamped data collected over time at no particular frequency. Time series data, however, is time-stamped data collected over time at a particular frequency. Some examples of time series data are: sales per month, trades per weekday, or Web site visits per hour. Businesses often want to analyze and understand transactional or time series data. Another common activity also includes building models for forecasting future behavior.

Unlike other data discussed in this book, time series data sets have a time dimension that must be considered. While so-called cross-sectional data, which can be used for building predictive models, typically features data created by or about humans, it is not unusual to find that time series data is created by devices or machines, such as sensors, in addition to human-generated data. The questions that arise from dealing with vast amounts of time series are typically different from what have been discussed earlier. Some of these questions will be discussed in this chapter.

It is important to note that time series data is a large component to the big data now being generated. There is a great opportunity to enhance data marts used for predictive modeling with attributes derived from time series data, which can improve accuracy of models. This new availability of data and potential improvement in models is very similar to the idea of using unstructured data in the context of predictive modeling.

There are many different methods available for the analyst who wants to go ahead and take advantage of time series data mining. High-performance data mining and big data analytics will certainly boost interest and success stories of this exciting and evolving area. After all, we are not necessarily finding lots of new attributes in big data but similar attributes to what already existed, measured more frequently—in other words, the time dimension will rise in importance. In this chapter, we focus on two important areas of time series data mining: dimension reduction and pattern detection.

REDUCING DIMENSIONALITY

The main purpose of dimension reduction techniques is to come up with a condensed representation of the information provided in a time series for further analysis. Instead of looking at the original data directly, new data is created that consists of many fewer observations but contains the most important features of the original data. The point of dimension reduction is that the original data may feature too many observations or points, which make it almost impossible to deal with in an efficient and timely manner. As an example, think of a sensor on a wind turbine that constantly streams information. An engineer might not be interested in constantly monitoring this information but wants to determine seasonal or trend patterns to improve power generation or predict needed maintenance before the turbine goes offline due to a part failure. Another example in the case of sales data is that a predictive model for cross-selling opportunities might become more accurate if a modeler can include buying behavior over time instead of static statistics, such as total money spent.

An easy-to-understand example of dimension reduction is commonly called seasonal analysis and typically is applied to transactional data. In order to reduce the original transactional data, statistics such as mean, minimum, or maximum are calculated at each point over a seasonal cycle (e.g., four quarters, 12 months, etc.). Depending on the seasonal cycle of choice, the amount of data can be reduced quite dramatically to just a few points. As you can see, this type of idea can be extended to time series data as well and to almost every time series analysis idea. Classical time series decomposition can be used in a similar fashion to derive components such as trend, cycles, or seasonality from time series data. Another easy and simple dimension reduction technique using descriptive statistics is a piecewise aggregate approximation (PAA) method, which is a binning-type dimension reduction of time series. For example, the time axis will be binned and the mean or median within each bin is calculated, and then the series of means or medians will be the reduced new time series. Again, these statistics can be used as input for further analysis, such as segmentation or predictive modeling. In the case of building predictive models for churn analysis, information like downward-trending sales patterns can be useful attributes for building more accurate models.

So far I have mainly used descriptive statistics for dimension reduction, which might filter out too much information. You may be wondering if it would be more appropriate to create new time series with fewer points instead, points that reflect the overall shape of original series. In other words, is it possible to represent the original time series as a combination of well-understood basic functions, such as straight lines or trigonometric functions? Examples of such approaches that include discrete Fourier transformation (DFT), discrete wavelet transformation (DWT), or singular value decomposition (SVD). DFT, for example, represents time series as a linear combination of sines and cosines but keeps only the first few coefficients. This allows us to represent the information of a time series with fewer points—but the main features of the time series will be kept.

DETECTING PATTERNS

The second area is pattern detection in time series data. This area can be divided into two subareas: finding patterns within a time series and finding patterns across many time series. These techniques are used quite successfully for voice recognition using computers, where the data can be represented as time series reflecting sound waves.

Let us start with an example for finding patterns within a time series: When analyzing streaming data collected from sensors, you may want to find patterns that indicate ill behavior of a system. If such patterns can be detected, an engineer could use this information to monitor a system and prevent future failures if the pattern starts to occur. This is the underlying concept of what sometimes is called predictive maintenance: Engineers try to determine problems before they occur—outside of scheduled maintenance activities.

When faced with many time series, the idea of pattern detection can be extended to address questions like: Which time series indicate similar behavior? Which time series indicates unusual behavior? And finally, given a time series of interest, which of the many other series is most similar to this target series? Similarity analysis is the method of choice for coping with these types of questions.

Similarity analysis, as the name suggests, can be used to measure the similarity between time series. It is a very useful analysis that can be applied for clustering or classifying time series which vary in length or timing. Two very prominent application areas are fraud detection and new product forecasting.

Fraud Detection

Credit card providers are using similarity analysis to automate the detection of fraudulent behavior in financial transactions. They are interested in spotting exceptions to average behavior by comparing many detailed time series against a known pattern of abusive behavior.

New Product Forecasting

New product forecasting for consumer goods manufacturers and retailers is a constant challenge. The situations include predicting entirely new types of products, new markets for existing products (such as expanding a regional brand nationally or globally), and refinements of existing products (such as "new and improved" versions or packaging changes). All require a forecast of future sales without historic data for the new product. However, by using techniques such as similarity analysis, an analyst can examine the demand patterns of past new products having similar attributes and identify the range of demand curves that can be used to model demand for the new product.

In a way, similarity analysis can be thought of as an extension of techniques based on distance measures. If you want to determine routes between cities, you first need to create a matrix of distances that measure the distances between all cities of interest. When transitioning to apply this concept to time series, you are faced with the challenge of dealing with the dynamic nature of time series. Two series can feature the same shape but are of different length. In this case, standard distance measures cannot be applied. A similarity measure is a metric that measures the distance between time series while taking into account the ordering. Similarity measures can be computed between input series and target series, as well as similarity measures that "slide" the target sequence with respect to the input sequence. The slides can occur by observation index (sliding-sequence similarity measures) or by seasonal index (seasonal-sliding-sequence similarity measures).

These similarity measures can be used to compare a single input sequence to several other representative target sequences. For example, given a single input sequence, you can classify the input sequence by finding the "most similar" or "closest" target sequence. Similarity measures can also be computed between several sequences to form a similarity matrix. Clustering techniques can then be applied to the similarity matrix. This technique is used in time series clustering. When dealing with sliding similarity measures (observational or seasonal index), we can compare a single target sequence to subsequence pieces of many other input sequences on a sliding basis. This situation arises in time series analogies. For example, given a single target series, you can find the times in the history of the input sequence that are similar while preserving the seasonal indices.

In this chapter, we have been dealing with questions that are dynamic in nature and for which we are typically faced with so-called time series data. We looked at ways to handle the increased complexity introduced by the time dimension, and we focused mainly on dimension reduction techniques and pattern detection in time series data.

TIME SERIES DATA MINING IN ACTION: NIKE+ FUELBAND

Nike in 2006 began to release products from a new product called Nike+, beginning with the Nike+ iPod sensor to track exercise data into popular consumer devices. This product line of activity monitors has expanded quite a bit and currently covers integration with basketball shoes, running shoes, iPhones, Xbox Kinect, and wearable devices including the FuelBand.

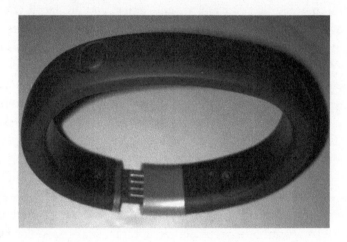

The Nike+ FuelBand is a wrist-worn bracelet device that contains a number of sensors to track users' activity. The monitoring of your activity causes you to be more active, which will help you achieve your fitness goals more easily. The idea of generating my own data to analyze and helping increase my fitness level was (and still is) very appealing to me, so I dropped as many subtle and not-so-subtle hints to my wife that this would make a great birthday present. I even went as far as to take my wife to the Nike Town store in midtown Manhattan to show her just how cool it was. She was tolerant but not overly impressed. I found out afterward that she had already ordered the FuelBand and was trying not to tip me off.

So for my birthday in 2012, I got a Nike+ FuelBand. I have faithfully worn it during my waking hours except for a ten-day period when I had to get a new one due to a warranty issue.[1] So to talk about how to deal

---

[1] Nike was great about replacing the device that was covered by warranty.

with times series data, I decided to use my activity data as captured on my Nike FuelBand. The first challenge in this was to get access to my data. Nike has a very nice Web site and iPhone app that let you see graphics and details of your activity through a day, but it does not let you answer some of the deeper questions that I wanted to understand, such as:

- Is there a difference in my weekend versus weekday activity?
- How does the season affect my activity level?
- Am I consistently as active in the morning, afternoon, and evening?
- How much sleep do I get on the average day?
- What is my average bedtime?

All of these questions and more were of great interest to me but not possible to answer without a lot of manual work or an automated way to get to the data. One evening I stumbled on the Nike+ developer's site. Nike has spent a good amount of time developing an application program interface (API) and related services so that applications can read and write data from the sensors. The company has a posted API that allows you to request data from a device that is associated with your account. For my account I have mileage from running with the Nike+ running app for iPhone and the Nike+ FuelBand. I went to the developer Web site and, using the forms there, I was able to play with the APIs and see some data. After hours of struggling, I sought out help from a friend who was able to write a script using Groovy to get the data in just an hour. This is an important idea to remember: In many cases, turning data into information is not a one-man show. It relies on a team of talented individual specialists who complement each other and round out the skills of the team. Most of the time spent on a modeling project is actually consumed with getting the data ready for analysis. Now that I had the data, it was time to explore and see what I could find. What follows is a set of graphics that show what I learned about my activity level according to the Nike+ FuelBand.

Seasonal Analysis

The most granular level of FuelBand data that can be requested through the API is recorded at the minute level. Using my data from September 2012 until October 2013, I created a data set with about

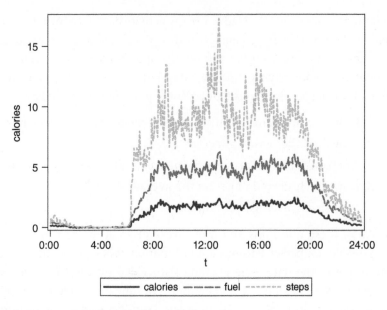

Figure 8.1 Seasonal Index of Authors Activity Levels

560,000 observations. One of the easiest ways to look into that kind of big-time data is seasonal analysis. Seasonal data can be summarized by seasonal index. For example, Figure 8.1 is obtained by hourly seasonal analysis.

From Figure 8.1, you can see that my day is rather routine. I usually become active shortly after 6:00 AM and ramp up my activity level until just before 9:00 AM, when I generally arrive at work. I then keep the same activity level through the business day and into the evening. Around 7:00 PM, I begin to ramp down my activity levels until I retire for the evening, which appears to happen around 12:00 to 1:00 AM. This is a very accurate picture of my typical day at a macro level. I have an alarm set for 6:30 AM on weekdays, and with four young children I am up by 7:00 AM most weekend mornings. I have a predictable morning routine that used to involve a five-mile run. The workday usually includes a break for lunch and brief walk, which show up as a small spike around 1:00 PM. My afternoon ramps down at 7:00 PM because that is when the bedtime routine starts for my children and my activity level drops accordingly.

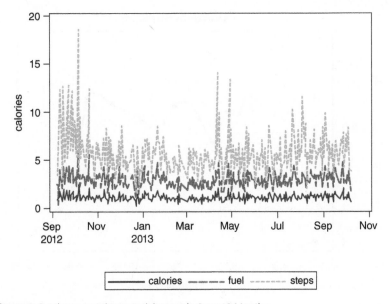

Figure 8.2 Minute-to-Minute Activity Levels Over 13 Months

Trend Analysis

Figure 8.2 shows my activity levels as a trend over 13 months. You can see the initial increase in activity as my activity level was gamified by being able to track it. There is also the typical spike in activity level that often occurs at the beginning of a new year and the commitment to be more active. There is also another spike in early May, as the weather began to warm up and my children participated in soccer, football, and other leagues that got me on the field and more active. In addition, the days were longer and allowed for more outside time. The trend stays high through the summer.

Similarity Analysis

Let us look at the data in a different way. Since the FuelBand is a continuous biosensor, an abnormal daily pattern can be detected (if any exists). This is the similarity search problem between target and input series that I mentioned earlier. I used the first two months of data to make a query (target) series, which is an hourly sequence averaged over two months. In other words, the query sequence is my average

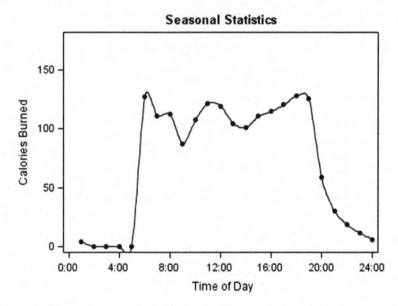

Figure 8.3 Average Pattern of Calories Burned over Two-Month Period

hourly pattern in a day. For example, Figure 8.3 shows my hourly pattern of calories burned averaged from 09SEP2012 to 9NOV2012.

Using the SIMULARITY procedure in SAS/ETS® to find my abnormal day based on calorie burn data.

Using dynamic time warping methods to measure the distance between two sequences, I found the five most abnormal days based on the initial patterns over the first two months of data compared to about 300 daily series from 10 Nov. 2012 to. This has many applications in areas such as customer traffic to a retail store or monitoring of network traffic for a company network.

From Table 8.1, you see that May 1, 2013, and April 29, 2013, were the two most abnormal days. This abnormal measure does not indicate I was not necessarily much more or less active but that the pattern of my activity was the most different from the routine I had established in the first two months. These two dates correspond to a conference, SAS Global Forum, which is the premier conference for SAS users. During the conference, I attended talks, met with customers, and demonstrated new product offerings in the software demo area.

Table 8.1 Top Five Days with the Largest Deviation in Daily Activity

Obs	Day Sequence	Distance to Baseline
1	ActDate_5_1_2013	30.5282
2	ActDate_4_29_2013	25.4976
3	ActDate_1_13_2013	18.6811
4	ActDate_8_22_2013	17.6915
5	ActDate_6_26_2013	16.6947

As you can see from Figures 8.4 and 8.5, my conference lifestyle is very different from my daily routine. I get up later in the morning. I am overall less active, but my activity level is higher later in the day.

For certain types of analysis, the abnormal behavior is of the most interest; for others, the similarity to a pattern is of the most interest. An example of abnormal patterns is the monitoring of chronically ill or elderly patients. With this type of similarity analysis, home-bound seniors could be monitored remotely and then have health care staff dispatched when patterns of activity deviate from an individual's norm.

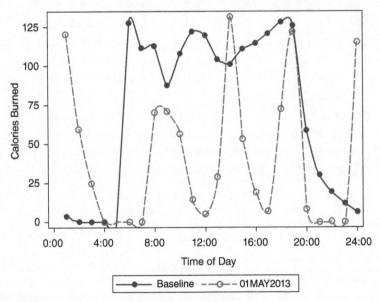

Figure 8.4 Comparison of Baseline Series and 01May2013

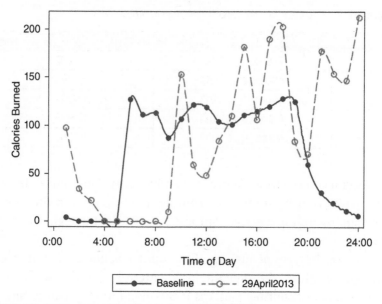

Figure 8.5 Comparison of Baseline Series and 29April2013

This method of similarity analysis is useful because each patient would have their own unique routine activity pattern that could be compared to their current day's activities. An example of pattern similarity is running a marathon. If you are trying to qualify for the Boston Marathon, you will want to see a pattern typical of other qualifiers when looking at your individual mile splits.[2] Figure 8.6 shows the two most similar days from my FuelBand data.

I have a seen a very strong trend to create wearable devices that collect consistent amounts of detailed data. A few examples include Progressive Insurance's Snapshot™ device, which collects telemetric data such as the speed, GPS location, rate of acceleration, and angle

---

[2] The Boston Marathon is the only marathon in the United States for which every participant must have met a qualifying time. The qualifying times are determined by your age and gender. I hope to qualify one day.

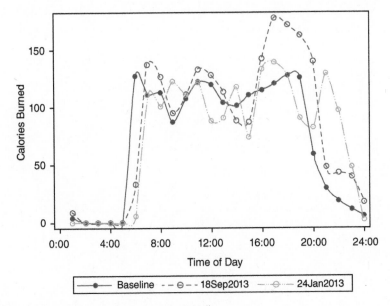

Figure 8.6 Two Most Similar Days to the Baseline

of velocity every 10 seconds while the car is running; or using smartphone GPS data to determine if a person might have Parkinson's disease, as the Michael J. Fox Foundation tried to discover in a Kaggle contest.[3]

---

[3] I am a huge fan of Kaggle and joined in the first weeks after the site came online. It has proven to be a great chance to practice my skills and ensure that the software I develop has the features to solve a large diversity of data mining problems. For more information on this and other data mining contests, see http://www.kaggle.com.

CHAPTER **9**

Recommendation Systems

If we have data, let's look at data. If all we have are opinions, let's go with mine.

—Jim Barksdale, former Netscape CEO

WHAT ARE RECOMMENDATION SYSTEMS?

Recommendation systems, also known as recommendation engines, are a type of information system whose purpose is to suggest, or recommend, items or actions to users. The recommendations may consist of retail items (movies, books, etc.) or actions, such as following other users in a social network. Typically, the suggestions are a small subset selected from a large collection, according to criteria such as preferences previously expressed by users. Other possible criteria include age, gender, and location.

The most common strategies followed by recommendation systems are the following.

■ **Content-based filtering** gathers auxiliary information (e.g., user demographics, music genre, keywords, answers to a questionnaire) to generate a profile for each user or item. Users are

163

matched to items based on their profiles. Example: Pandora's Music Genome Project.

■ **Collaborative filtering** is based on past user behavior. Each user's rating, purchasing, or viewing history allows the system to establish associations between users with similar behavior and between items of interest to the same users. Example: Netflix.

Collaborative filtering is perhaps the most popular of these strategies, due to its domain-free nature. Among collaborative filtering systems, one can further distinguish between neighborhood-based methods, based on user-user or item-item distances, and latent factor or reduced-dimension models, which automatically discover a small number of descriptive **factors** for users and items. Low-rank matrix factorization is the best-known example of reduced-dimension models and is among the most flexible and successful methods underlying recommendation systems.[1] There are many variants of matrix factorization, including probabilistic and Bayesian versions. Restricted Boltzmann machines, a type of deep learning neural network, are another state-of-the-art approach.

WHERE ARE THEY USED?

The scope of application for recommendation systems is vast. Any business that sells a wide variety of items to large numbers of people is a potential user of recommendation systems. They are employed by retailers, such as Amazon, Netflix, and Target; movie and music Web sites, such as Netflix and last.fm; and social networks like Facebook and Twitter. They can also be found in grocery stores, such as Tesco.

Besides the aforementioned examples in retail, media, and social networking, recommendation systems are employed by general-purpose Web sites, such as Yahoo! and Google, in order to select the best advertisements to serve to each user, based on browsing history and other information. Another application is **next-best offer** in marketing decision making, used for instance by Schwan's Foods for increasing sales of frozen food items.

---

[1] The rank of a matrix is the number of linearly independent columns the matrix contains.

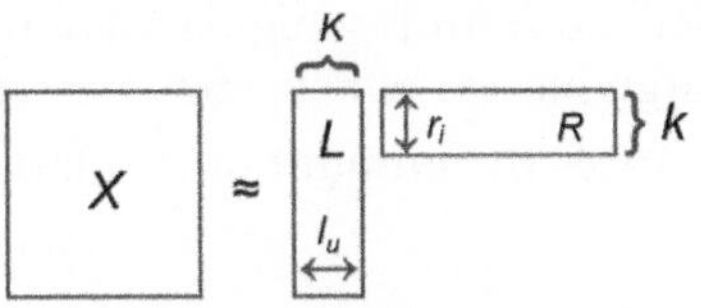

Figure 9.1 Factor Matrix

HOW DO THEY WORK?

We will describe the basic mathematical setting underlying most recommendation systems. Let the ratings be arranged as a matrix X with N_u rows and N_i columns, where N_u is the number of users and N_i is the number of items to be rated. The element x_{ui} of X is the rating given by user u to item i. Typically, we know only the values for a few elements of X. Let D denote the known ratings stored in the form of tuples $(u_1, i_1, x_{u_1 i_1}) \ldots (u_n, i_n, x_{u_n i_n})$, as illustrated in Figure 9.1. We assume there are n known ratings.

Baseline Model

A basic, "baseline" model is given by

$$x_{ui} = b_0 + b_u + b_i$$

where b_0, b_u and b_i are a global, user, and item bias terms, respectively. The b_0 term corresponds to the overall average rating, while b_u is the amount by which user u deviates, on average, from b_0. The same applies to b_i for item i. The goal is to estimate b_0, b_u, and b_i for all u and i, given D.

The bias terms can be estimated by solving the least squares optimization problem

$$\min_{b_u, b_i} \sum_{(u,i) \in D} (x_{ui} - b_0 - b_u - b_i)^2 + \lambda \left(\sum_u b_u^2 + \sum_i b_i^2 \right)$$

with b_0 set to the average of all known x_{ui}. The first term is the sum of squared errors between the observed ratings and the ratings predicted

Table 9.1 Data Set D of Known Ratings

u_1	i_1	$x_{u_1 i_1}$
	$\vdots$	
u_n	i_n	$x_{u_n i_n}$

by the model. The second term is a regularization penalty designed to discourage overly large biases, which are associated with overfitting. The parameter λ controls the amount of regularization.

Low-Rank Matrix Factorization

A more flexible model is given by low-rank matrix factorization. Consider the following inner product:

$$x_{ui} = l_u \times r_i$$

where l_u and r_i are vectors of dimension K. The aforementioned model can also be expressed by the matrix product.

$$X = LR$$

where

rows of L (the "left" factor matrix) = vectors l_u for all users

columns of the "right" factor matrix R = vectors r_i for all items

This is depicted in Figure 9.1. In this model, X has rank K, which is typically much lower than either N_u or N_i, hence the name low-rank matrix factorization.

L and R can be estimated by solving the optimization problem:

$$\min_{l_u, r_i} \sum_{(u,i) \in D} \left(x_{ui} - l_u \cdot r_i \right)^2 + \lambda \left(\sum_u \| l_u \|^2 + \sum_i \| r_i \|^2 \right)$$

which is similar to the baseline model. The regularization term avoids overfitting by penalizing the norms of the factors. Two popular methods for solving this problem are stochastic gradient descent and alternating least squares.

Stochastic Gradient Descent

Stochastic gradient descent starts from an initial guess for each l_u, r_i and proceeds by updating in the direction of the negative gradient of the objective, according to

$$l_u \leftarrow l_u - \eta(e_{ui} r_i - \lambda l_u)$$

$$r_i \leftarrow r_i - \eta(e_{ui} l_u - \lambda r_i)$$

where

$e_{ui} \triangleq x_{ui} - l_u.r_i$ = prediction error for the rating associated with the pair (u,i)

η = user-defined learning step size

The updates are made one rating at a time, with each pair (u,i) selected uniformly at random, without replacement, from the data set D. This is the reason behind the name "stochastic." Once a full pass through D (i.e., an epoch) is completed, the algorithm begins a new pass through the same examples, in a different random order. This is repeated until convergence, which typically requires multiple epochs.

Stochastic gradient descent does not require the full data set to be stored in memory, which is an important advantage when D is very large.

Alternating Least Squares

Another well-known method is alternating least squares, which proceeds in two steps. First, it solves Equation 1 with respect to the left factors l_u by fixing the right factors r_i; then it solves for the r_i with the l_u fixed. Each of these steps can be tackled by a standard least squares solver. Define n_u as the number of ratings from user u and $R[u]$ as the restriction of R to the items rated by u. Let also the vector x_u denote the ratings given by u, in the same order as in $R[u]$. Then the estimate of l_u is found by solving

$$\begin{bmatrix} R[u] \\ \sqrt{\lambda n_u} I_K \end{bmatrix} l_u = \begin{bmatrix} x_u \\ 0 \end{bmatrix}$$

where I_K is the $K \times K$ identity matrix. The estimate of r_i is analogous.

Alternating least squares has the advantage of being simpler to parallelize than stochastic gradient descent. It has the disadvantage of larger memory requirements. The entire data set needs to be stored in memory, which can be an issue for large D.

Restricted Boltzmann Machines

There exist many other recommendation approaches besides low-rank matrix factorization. In this section we address restricted Boltzmann machines (RBMs), due to their growing popularity and the fact that

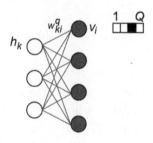

Figure 9.2 Restricted Boltzmann Machine for One User

they represent a distinctive and highly competitive approach. An RBM is a two-layer neural network with stochastic units. The name "restricted" comes from the fact that the units must be arranged in a bipartite graph, as shown in Figure 9.2. Units in the visible layer are connected only to units in the hidden layer, and vice versa. The connections are undirected, meaning that the network can operate in both directions, with the hidden units exciting the visible units and vice versa.

In the recommendation setting, there exists a separate RBM for each user u. Assuming that user u has rated m items, there are m visible units in the corresponding network.

The output of the k-th hidden unit is typically binary and is denoted h_k with $k = 1, \ldots, K$. The output of the i-th visible unit is v_i with $i = 1, \ldots, m$. For recommendation, v_i is usually ordinal with discrete values between 1 and Q. The q-th value of v_i, denoted v_i^q, has a certain probability of being activated (i.e., the network estimates a probability distribution over all possible values of v_i). The connection between the k-th hidden unit and the q-th value of the i-th visible unit is associated with a weight w_{ki}^q. To avoid clutter, bias terms are not shown in Figure 9.2. The dependence on user u is also omitted.

The units are stochastic in the sense that the output obeys a probability distribution conditioned on the input rather than being a deterministic function of the input. The hidden units are binary with

$$p(h_k = 1 \mid v) = \sigma\left(b_k + \sum_{i=1}^{m} \sum_{q=1}^{Q} v_i^q w_{ki}^q \right)$$

where
b_k = a bias term
$\sigma(x) = 1/(1 + e^{-x})$ = a sigmoid function

The ordinal visible units follow a softmax rule:

$$p\left(v_i^q = 1 | h\right) = \frac{\exp\left(b_i^q + \sum_{k=1}^{K} h_k w_{ki}^q\right)}{\sum_{l=1}^{Q} \exp\left(b_i^l + \sum_{k=1}^{K} h_k w_{ki}^l\right)}$$

with bias term b_i^q. All user-specific networks share connection weights and bias terms when multiple users rate the same item, but both hidden and visible units have distinct states for each user.

Contrastive Divergence

The parameters of an RBM are the weights and biases. These are learned by maximizing the marginal log-likelihood of the visible units, given by

$$p(V) = \sum_h \frac{\exp(-E(V,h))}{\sum_{V',h'} \exp(-E(V',h'))}$$

with the term $E(V,h)$ representing the "energy" for the network configuration. This has the expression

$$E(V,h) = -\sum_{i=1}^{m} \sum_{k=1}^{K} \sum_{q=1}^{Q} w_{ki}^q h_k v_i^q + \sum_{i=1}^{m} \log Z_i - \sum_{i=1}^{m} \sum_{q=1}^{Q} v_i^q b_i^q - \sum_{k=1}^{K} h_k b_k$$

where Z_i is a normalizing constant. Learning is performed by gradient ascent of $\log p(V)$. The updates for the weights are

$$w_{ki}^q \leftarrow w_{ki}^q + \epsilon \frac{\partial \log p(V)}{\partial w_{ki}^q}$$

$$\frac{\partial \log p(V)}{\partial w_{ki}^q} = \langle v_i^q h_j \rangle_{data} - \langle v_i^q h_j \rangle_{model}$$

where $\langle \cdot \rangle$ denotes the expectation operator. The biases follow similar updates. The term $\langle v_i^q h_j \rangle_{data}$ is equal to the frequency with which the binary quantities h_j and v_i^q are simultaneously on when the network is being driven by the data set D, meaning that the visible units v_i^q are clamped to the values in the training set. The term $\langle v_i^q h_j \rangle_{model}$ is the expectation with respect to the distribution of v_i^q defined by the learned model, and it is far harder to calculate. For this reason, an approximation is used. In the Monte Carlo–based contrastive divergence method, the approximation is

$$\langle v_i^q h_j \rangle_T \approx \langle v_i^q h_j \rangle_{model}$$

where $\langle v_i^q h_j \rangle_T$ denotes the expectation over T steps of a Gibbs sampler.

As seen, for example, in the Netflix competition, RBMs tend to perform well for cases where matrix factorization has difficulties, and vice versa. For this reason, a successful approach consists of utilizing both a matrix factorization recommender and an RBM in tandem, thus providing a combined prediction.

ASSESSING RECOMMENDATION QUALITY

The best metric for evaluating a recommender system depends on the problem at hand. In the majority of applications, the root mean square error (RMSE) is the measure of choice. The RMSE is defined as

$$RMSE = \sqrt{\frac{1}{n} \sum_{(u,i) \in D} (x_{ui} - l_u . r_i)^2}$$

and it measures the numerical discrepancy between the actual and predicted value for x_{ui}. Moreover, the RMSE is directly related to the data fit term in Equation 1, which means that it is the metric being optimized in most matrix factorization schemes. A similar relationship exists with the log-likelihood objective optimized in RBMs.

In some situations, the rank ordering of the recommendations may matter more than the specific predicted values for x_{ui}. For such cases, when a list of the top r recommendations is desired, it may be preferable to use a measure derived from information retrieval, such as the mean average precision at r, denoted $MAP@r$. This is defined for a set of N_u users as

$$MAP@r = \frac{1}{N_u} \sum_{u=1}^{N_u} AP_u @r$$

$$AP_u @r = \frac{1}{\#relevant_u} \sum_{k=1}^{r} P_u @k \times I_{u,k}$$

in which $AP_u@r$ is the average precision at r for user u. The precision at k, written as $P_u@k$, is the fraction of items in the top k results that are relevant for user u. The indicator variable $I_{u,k}$ is equal to 1 if item k is relevant for user u, and 0 otherwise. The total number of relevant items for this user is denoted $\#relevant_u$.

The $MAP@r$ is difficult to optimize directly. For this reason, approximations and upper bounds are often used. It is known that optimizing for the RMSE and then sorting the items in descending order of predicted x_{ui} is equivalent to minimizing one such upper bound.

RECOMMENDATIONS IN ACTION: SAS LIBRARY

The library at SAS keeps records of users, books, book requests, and renewals. As an application example, we applied low-rank matrix factorization in order to predict whether a given user will request or renew a particular book. The data set contains 8180 records pertaining to 2212 users and 6763 books. The number of renewals ranges from 0 to 23. We have added 1 to the number of renewals, in order to differentiate between books that have only been requested once and missing data. Hence, the "rating" in the postprocessed data set ranges from 1 to 24.

Note that the observed entries constitute an extremely sparse subset of the unknown full matrix X; only $\dfrac{8180}{2212 \times 6763} \approx 0.05\%$ of X is observed.

We utilized $K = 20$ factors and ran stochastic gradient descent (following Equation 2) for 40 epochs using a randomly selected fraction of the data set training. The remainder was held out in order to assess testing error. The computation took only a few seconds on a standard desktop computer. The resulting RMSE is plotted in Figure 9.3.

Rather than trying to predict the number of renewals for a user/book pair, which is not necessarily a useful task per se, it may be of interest to recommend a list of r books to a given user u. In order to do so, it is possible to compute estimates $\hat{x}_{ui} = l_u \cdot r_i$ for all books i and sort the list of $\hat{x}_{ui}$ in descending order. The top r entries correspond to the recommended books. Note that we do not report the $MAP@r$ metric, since that would require a reliable mechanism for inferring whether each recommended book is relevant for each user.

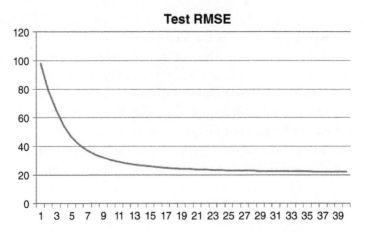

Figure 9.3 Root Mean Square Error on a Held-Out Test Set from SAS Library Data

As a concrete example, we examine a specific user in the data set. The random subset of entries utilized for training is shown in Table 9.2. The top 10 recommendations generated for this user by the matrix factorization model are shown in Table 9.3. It is apparent that the model has captured the user's interest in linear regression and econometric themes.

Table 9.2 Training Entries for a Specific User

Book ID	Text
660	Logistic regression examples using the SAS system.
3890	The complete guide to option pricing formulas / Espen Gaarder Haug.
6304	The geometry of multivariate statistics / Thomas D. Wickens.
4691	Generalized additive models / T.J. Hastie, R.J. Tibshirani.
4674	Survival analysis : techniques for censored and truncated data / John P. Klein, Melvin L. Moeschberger.
20101	Practical methods for design and analysis of complex surveys / Risto Lehtonen, Erkki Pahkinen.
21353	Bayesian ideas and data analysis an introduction for scientists and statisticians / Ronald Christensen, Wesley Johnson, Adam Branscum, Timothy Hanson.
13287	Matrices with applications in statistics / Franklin A. Graybill.
6214	Generalized linear models / P. McCullagh, J.A. Nelder.

13628	Kendall's advanced theory of statistics. Vol. 1, Distribution theory / Alan Stuart, J. Keith Ord.
3476	Sampling of populations : methods and applications / Paul S. Levy, Stanley Lemeshow.
4675	Data : a collection of problems from many fields for the student and research worker / D.F. Andrews, A.M. Herzberg.
18210	Generalized linear models for insurance data / Piet de Jong, Gillian Z. Heller.
18971	Computer intensive statistical methods : validation model selection and bootstrap / J.S. Urban Hjorth.
18924	Applied linear statistical models : regression, analysis of variance, and experimental designs / John Neter, William Wasserman
19765	Sampling : design and analysis / Sharon L. Lohr.
19765	Sampling : design and analysis / Sharon L. Lohr.
20649	Bayesian methods : a social and behavioral sciences approach / Jeff Gill.
23286	Analysis of health surveys / Edward L. Korn, Barry I. Graubard.
21148	Design and analysis of experiments with SAS / John Lawson.

Table 9.3 Top 10 Recommendations for the Specific User

Book ID	Text
6139	Econometric analysis / William H. Greene.
4165	The SAS system information delivery for the pharmaceutical industry.
5182	Estimation and inference in econometrics / Russell Davidson, James G. MacKinnon.
3951	Communication skills to inspire confidence / Barrie Hopson, Mike Scally.
19741	Statistical programming in SAS / A. John Bailer.
1011	Generalized linear models : a Bayesian perspective / edited by Dipak K. Dey, Sujit K. Ghosh, Bani K. Mallick.
6444	The Dilbert principle cubicle's-eye view of bosses, meetings, management fads & other workplace afflictions / Scott Adams.
23234	Multiple comparisons and multiple tests using SAS / Peter H. Westfall, Randall D. Tobias, Russell D. Wolfinger.
23305	Generalized linear models and extensions / James Hardin, Joseph Hilbe.
20712	Mathematical statistics / Jun Shao.

CHAPTER 10

Text Analytics

U nstructured data, of which text data is a major part, is one of the three major sources for the data volume explosion that has occurred in the last dozen years.[1] Nearly all of your communication is now in a digital format from email to tweets and blogs.[2] I was even able recently to change my phone plan, purchase a different high-speed Internet service, and correct a billing problem all via instant message chat session. Even when the communication happens via phone, it is likely being converted to a text format for storage and further potential analysis.

Text data, no matter the origin, presents challenges to process it and convert it from a raw form to make it suitable for modeling.

Working with text, or unstructured data, is one of the two major reasons that this area offers such a competitive advantage in many

---

*The data analysis for this chapter was generated using SAS Text Miner software, Version 13.1 of the SAS System for Windows. Copyright © 2013 SAS Institute Inc. SAS and all other SAS Institute Inc. product or service names are registered trademarks or trademarks of SAS Institute Inc., Cary, NC, USA.

[1] The other two sources are machine-to-machine data and images (which includes videos).

[2] This includes voice calls because they are digital and can be programmatically converted to text.

markets. It is sometimes very difficult to manipulate the data into a usable form. The recommended steps for getting data ready include:

- **Identify the problem you are trying to solve.** This may sound simple, but many projects fail because they do not have a clear scope and outcome and then they drift out of control until they are never heard from again.

- **Identify the potential sources of your data.** If this is purely text analytics, then sources will be unstructured. If this is predictive modeling, then this will likely include both structured and unstructured sources.

INFORMATION RETRIEVAL

Information retrieval is a needed action in almost any text analytics activity. Several activities are common tools in performing information retrieval:

- **File crawling.** File crawling is the process of recursively moving through files in order to extract the useful information for a later purpose. A common example is the archive folders created by Microsoft Outlook or folders for documentation or memos. The file types that have been identified, by either the crawler or the user, are noted and tagged for later information retrieval activities like text extraction.

- **Web crawling.** Web crawling is similar to file crawling except the activity takes place on the Web. Many people are familiar with the term "bots," software applications that perform automated and repetitive tasks. Scraping text from Web pages is one application of a bot. The Internet, because of its open standard protocol, makes conversion of Web pages to text straightforward. With so much of the human-generated data being text, Web crawling is an essential operation for getting information about what customers are thinking for competitive intelligence, managing brand reputation, and assessing community awareness to organizational initiatives.

- **Text extraction.** Text extraction is normally the step directly following Web or file crawling. It normally involves separating the text from the formatting of a document or Web page. An example would be the extraction of plain text from a Portable Document Format (PDF) file. Text extraction removes all of the formatting, font, and size type of information and leaves only the plain text for analysis.

- **Index and search.** In this age of the Internet, index and search are frequent occurrences. The information retrieval services must build indexes that can be used to facilitate effective search. In 2008, Google on its official blog said it had hit the milestone of identifying 1 trillion unique URLs at one time. With a quality index in place, users can then search not only for a single term but also perform a facilitated search that includes rules like Boolean logic.

CONTENT CATEGORIZATION

Content categorization is the process of evaluating documents and suggesting or assigning categories based on their content. This can be done with several methods, but the most common is the bag-of-words method. It works much as it sounds. The words from a document are figuratively all placed into a bag and then they are drawn out in sets. The likelihood of words occurring together helps in classifying documents into categories based on the co-occurrence of words. Consider words like "river," "stream," and "bay"; they are likely to be found together in documents about water, but they might also be found in documents published by the Environmental Protection Agency (EPA) about pollution and contamination levels.

There are two main methods within content categorization: text topic identification and text clustering. In text topic creation, the words that make a document unique are compared to the words from other documents, and a similarity score is calculated. As more documents are measured and determined to be similar, topics emerge organically, without predefined direction or rules. Every document is given a score for every text topic, and then a cutoff value is applied to identify which documents belong to a particular topic. Documents can be found in multiple topics. Referring back to the water words in the previous paragraph, if there was topic on boats and EPA pollution, that document might be found in both topics because of the unique words. Text clustering, in contrast, limits documents to only one cluster. The clustering techniques are similar to those discussed in Chapter 6 on segmentation with the prestep of needing to convert the text to condensed numeric representation. This is often done using singular value decomposition (SVD). The SVD is similar to principal components in that it represents a compact numeric representation for a set of data.

Another key component for content categorization to be effective is the dictionary and thesaurus available to reduce the considered words to those that are relevant for differentiation. This means words that are common to all the documents will be eliminated or have reduced weight for classifying topics and clustering. This can also include words commonly found in the English language, such as "and," "to," "the," and so on.

In most organizations, it is necessary to obtain information about, and from, unstructured data that is created internally and externally. Taxonomists might develop the categories and concepts while subject matter experts write rules.

The process of categorizing content includes large, complex, and hierarchical taxonomies. Content categorization uses advanced linguistic technologies to identify metadata in, and about, your documents improve the business value of information technology and the corporate data that it manages. Content categorization is the automated process of classification and extraction of entities from input documents.

You will improve results on information retrieval and organization costs when all of the information created by, or within, your organization can be classified and easily retrieved.

TEXT MINING

Text mining is a discipline that combines data mining and text analytics to use unstructured or textual data along with structured data for the purposes of exploration, discovery, and predictive modeling or classification. Given a large body of textual data, it is desirable to know what main ideas are present. Being able to sift through large volumes of data requires the ability to successfully parse and filter text in order to reveal the most meaningful and significant content contained therein. One of the major obstacles to using unstructured data is summarizing it in a form that is usable for topic discovery and predictive modeling. Like most other data mining processes, textual data can require additional preparation to be effective in subsequent analysis.

Due to the many ways words can be represented (e.g., inflection), parsing such content requires the ability to be language aware. While English words are commonly separated by spaces, a language such as Mandarin does not use spaces in this way and thus impacts how tokenization is performed. Identifying different parts of speech plays a significant role in text mining as knowing how a word is used impacts further processing. For example, the term "bank" can mean a financial institution or a riverbed, depending on the context, but can also refer to the notion of wagering. Parsing techniques such as the use of synonyms can aid in treating different words as equivalent terms while stemming can reduce all forms of a term to its root (e.g., "improves," "improved," and "improving" reduces to "improve").

Filtering textual data eliminates content that is not applicable by reducing the total number of terms and documents used for analysis, all while preserving what is considered to be the most valuable and relevant content. Data can be reduced to capture a subset of documents that are relevant to a particular issue, which can significantly reduce the time and computational resources required for later analysis. Term and frequency weightings may be used to vary the importance of terms based on how frequently the terms occur in individual documents as well as across the entire collection of documents. A term may occur frequently in a given document while also occurring just as frequently in all of the other documents. Thus, this term is not a good discriminator in differentiating between documents and can be weighted accordingly. Other filters, such as spell correction, may also be required.

Learning the main themes of what a body of text is about is known as topic discovery. Through the use of various mathematical techniques (e.g., singular value decomposition [SVD], latent Dirichlet allocation [LDA]), the most significant and distinctive features of the text can be surfaced and enable seeing what terms and phrases best describe what is happening in the text. Using the same techniques, predictive modeling can take these same features and produce classifiers that can be used on unforeseen data that can accurately predict the target outcome. Using these data-driven, statistical-based models, classifiers can be trained, tested, and validated from any collection of text.

TEXT ANALYTICS IN ACTION: LET'S PLAY *JEOPARDY!*

If you have gotten to this point in the book, you probably have a good a strong impression that I am a really big nerd.[3] One of the nerdy behaviors I enjoy is trivia, and there is no better trivia game than watching *Jeopardy!* To those who are not familiar with the game, it is a quiz show format with three contestants and host Alex Trebek. The game takes place in a 30-minute TV time slot and has three sections, Jeopardy!, Double Jeopardy!, and Final Jeopardy!. Inexplicably my wife developed a real interest in *Jeopardy!* during her second pregnancy, which gave me a chance to indulge daily in a favorite pastime.

The Jeopardy! round presents the contestants with five distinct categories and five clues with each clue being assigned a dollar value beginning at $200 up to $1000.[4] (See Figure 10.1.) Each day there

Statistics History	Less is Moore	Fischer of Men	"Box"ing	Nonfiction Writers
100	100	100	100	100
200	200	200	200	200
300	300	300	300	300
400	400	400	400	400
500	500	500	500	500

Figure 10.1 *Jeopardy!* Game Board

---

[3] This is a badge I can wear proudly now that nerds are cool.

[4] The value of the individual clues has changed over time.

are three contestants, including two new contestants and the winner from the game the previous day. The winner is on the far left from the TV viewers' perspective, and two new players are in the center and far right. The round begins with the returning player selecting the first clue.

Now, one twist on *Jeopardy!* that distinguishes it from other quiz programs is that instead of giving the contestants a question, the contestants are given an answer and they must give the question to receive credit. For example, if the category is City Name Origins, the information presented to the contestants might be "It's the place in England where the oxen forded the river Thames." After the question is read, contestants race to press a hand-held buzzer. The fastest contestant to buzz in gets the opportunity to answer. However, remember that the response must be phrased as a question for the contestant to get points. For this question, the contestant must say, "What is Oxford?" If the contestant answers correctly, the value of the clue is credited to his or her total. That contestant then has control of the board and gets to select the next clue.

If the contestant answers the question incorrectly, the value of the clue is deducted from his or her total (amounts can go negative) and the remaining contestants have an opportunity to answer. Contestants only have one attempt per question, and they are allowed five seconds to respond once they have buzzed in to respond to the clue. If no contestant answers the question, the contestant who selected that clue retains control of the board. One additional twist to the game is that in the Jeopardy! and Double Jeopardy! rounds, certain clues are a "daily double."[5] This clue can be answered only by the contestant who selected it, and that contestant can wager any sum, up to either the current value of his or her account or $500, whichever is greater.[6] If contestants answer correctly, the amount they wagered is added to their total. If they answer incorrectly, the amount is deducted from their total, at which point they can have a negative account balance.

---

[5] One clue in the Jeopardy round and two in the Double Jeopardy round.

[6] The daily double has changed the outcome of many *Jeopardy!* games.

The Double Jeopardy! round is played just like the Jeopardy! round with the exception that clue values are doubled and there are two daily doubles.

The final round, called Final Jeopardy!, includes only a single question. Before the question is read, contestants are told the category, and then they must decide their wager based on their earnings to this point in the game. (Players with negative winnings after Double Jeopardy! are excluded from Final Jeopardy!.) The wager is not revealed to the audience or the other contestants at this point. After the wager is written, the question is revealed to the contestants, and they are given 15 seconds to record their response. After time expires, the response and wagers are revealed and the contestants' account balances are adjusted according to if they responded correctly to the clue. The contestant with the most money is named the winner and banks that money along with the invitation to return the next day and play again. The nonwinners are given a nominal parting gift.

Ken Jennings holds a number of Jeopardy! records including the most consecutive wins (74) and has earned over $3 million on the show. Jennings and others maintain the J! Archive Web site (www .j-archive.com). This Web site has an archive of all the clues, responses, and contestants ever to play Jeopardy! Because of the show's long run, that amounts to about 250,000 questions.

It is because of the popularity of the game show, its approachability, and its data volume that I wanted to showcase it here to discuss text analytics methods and the power of this capability. Jeff Stewart, a friend of mine, is a former Jeopardy! contestant (he won a car!), and we began to engage in a discussion of how to prepare for the game show. He mentioned the fact that to maximize your preparation, you need to know which topics require deep knowledge (U.S. Presidents) and which ones require only rudimentary knowledge (Chinese philosophers). This sparked my curiosity to try to quantify what topics give you the best value for your time.

This problem, like almost all real-world analytics problems, starts with getting the data into a usable form. The text analytics suite from SAS was used for all of this analysis, but I have written the steps so that they could be generically followed independent of the software used.

Information Retrieval Steps

The first step is to collect the data from the source. In this case I used the Web crawler to recursively download the data from each game stored at J! Archive. J! Archive has a single page for each game, and that page includes a wealth of information including all the clues, their point values, who answered correctly and incorrectly, what order the questions were selected, and more.

With the data downloaded, I needed to identify the different parts of the HTML files and create metadata (data about the data) for later analysis. In the case of the *Jeopardy!* questions, the attributes I tagged were game ID, question text, subject, dollar value, answer, and so on.

In text analytics, "document" is a generic term to mean a single entity. During the analysis, "document" was at times used to refer to a game and other times to a clue.

After the entities had been tagged and extracted from the HTML files, they were assembled in an XML form in chronological order across all games. In the next code snippet, you can see how the details for a single clue are represented and the custom tags used to identify the different parts of the data.

Excerpt from XML file of Text Parsing from J! Archive

```
<clue>
    <game_id>329</game_id>
    <show_number>4782</show_number>
    <text>Sure, you studied presidents & state birds, but
    how the Beastie Boys & their "No Sleep Till" here</
    text>
    <value>$1000</value>
    <order_number>15</order_number>
    <correct_response>Brooklyn</correct_response>
    <is_daily_double>False</is_daily_double>
    <daily_double>-1.000000</daily_double>
    <dialogue/>
    <is_triple_stumper>False</is_triple_stumper>
    <row_index>2</row_index>
    <category>U.S. GEOGRAPHY IN SONG</category>
    -<answers>
            -<correct>
                    <name>Ken</name>
            </correct>
    </answers>
</clue>
```

These steps of preparing the data were common to all the analysis questions for this example.

Discovering Topics in *Jeopardy!* Clues

Primary themes or ideas existing within a given body of text can be automatically discovered using the text analytics techniques discussed in this section. Through automatic term and document association and by using SVD techniques, the most meaningful and significant features emerge and describe the overall topics occurring in the corpus.[7]

The J! Archive data set has a number of text fields that can be used for topic discovery, but the most useful in this data is the clue text. The clue text is the most meaningful for distinguishing topics occurring over all *Jeopardy!* games. In general, the largest field yields the most textual information.

Building on the data processing information from the Information Retrieval section, topics can now be learned. As a starting point, I requested that 25 topics be created from the clues. The top four categories along with the most common terms used to define each category and how many clues were found under that topic are shown in Table 10.1.

If you have seen the show, these topics are not surprising, but the information could not have been captured by looking at the clue categories. In *Jeopardy!* the clue categories generally provide insight into the correct response. As an example here is a clue: "On '50s TV he played the man with badge 714." This might be obvious to some as a *Dragnet* reference but to many it might not be. Using the category of "Jack's in the box," you have the additional information that the person's name includes "Jack"; the answer in this case is of course Jack Webb. Another example is the clue "This *NSYNC song hit the top 5 in 2000; see ya!" Unless you are a major fan of boy bands, this song title is probably not on the tip of your tongue, but coupled with the category of "Say that 3 times" I think a number of people can correctly answer "Bye Bye Bye." Other examples of categories that provide meaning for the clue response but not the topic are "When you're having fun, "Watcha doin'," "Rhyme hole," and so on. (See Table 10.2.)

---

[7] A corpus is a large and structured set of texts.

TEXT ANALYTICS ◀ 185

Table 10.1 Most Common Topics from *Jeopardy!* Clues

Topic	Common Terms	Number of Clues
Music	Song	11,264
	Hit	
	Hear	
	Group	
	Sing	
Literature	Write	10,976
	Novel	
	Book	
	Author	
	Play	
Water Geography	Large	10,144
	World	
	Island	
	Mile	
	Lake	
Television	Play	9,743
	TV	
	Show	
	Game	
	Movie	

Knowing the most popular topics asked on *Jeopardy!* is an important advantage as you study and prepare to play the game. The number of questions asked in any one game comes from a very wide body of knowledge. If you encounter a category in which you have limited knowledge, it could end your winning streak (or stop it from getting

Table 10.2 Top-Scoring Questions from the Music Topic

Clue	Category
Frank Sinatra despised this 1966 hit, calling it the worst song he'd ever heard..."Doo-be-doo-be-doo"	Song Standards
In song it's "A Name I Call Myself"	2-Letter Words
Hop-happy song: 99 B O B O T W	*Jeopardy!* Ditloids
In a 1978 song he was "Slip Slidin' Away"	Sliding
Steve Miller had a No. 2 hit with this 1977 song	Song Birds

started). Using a text topic approach, you have information on which topics are the most likely to be asked so that you can use your study time efficiently. This has common application in business as well. The ability to quickly and accurately identify the topic of a customer question either through a customer call center or electronic communication will improve an organization's chances to address the customer's specific concern and therefore improve retention and customer profitability.

These topics were used in a very raw form to show the ability of text analytics techniques to organize information. In practice, examination and refinement of the topics would likely be needed.

Topics from Clues Having Incorrect or Missing Answers

Building on the previous sections of preparing the data and identifying the most common topics, it would be useful to know if there are certain topics that contestants are not prepared for and then provide a strategic advantage in your ability to answer questions other contestants cannot. Alternatively, we might discover that contestants answer incorrectly in a somewhat uniform pattern and no advantage can be gained.

To address this question, the unstructured data of the clue must be combined with structured information about the contestants and their responses to the clues. An incorrect answer was defined as a clue when any contestant provided an incorrect answer or where all three contestants failed to provide any answer. There are around 31,000 questions (about 18%) answered incorrectly by at least one contestant.

Repeating the same analysis to identify clue topics, using this subset of questions allows the comparison to see if contestants are ill prepared for certain topics or if there are holes in the contestants' knowledge of the most popular clue topics. The two most popular topics of the questions with a wrong answer are shown in Table 10.3. The most common topic for missed questions is clues that might have multiple answers and the contestant needs to know the dates of events to select the correct response. As an example, "This single-named Renaissance artist who died in 1520 was regarded in the 19th century as the greatest painter ever." There are four single-named Renaissance painters that most people know (largely because of the Teenage Mutant Ninja Turtles), but contestants must know which one died in 1520, and if there is more than one, they must also know which was named the greatest painter ever in the 19th century.

Table 10.3 Most Popular Topics for Questions with a Wrong Answer

Topic	Common Terms	Number of Clues
Century Events	Century	2,505
	19th	
	Work	
	Famous	
	Born	
Music	Song	2,297
	Hit	
	Hear	
	Group	
	First	

This question is difficult because while Raphael is the only one of the four to die in 1520, Leonardo da Vinci died in 1519 so without a high degree of certainty it would be easy to respond incorrectly.

The percentage of questions missed varies from topic to topic but with the exception of Century Events, they are all within a few percentage points of the overall missed question rate, and there is no statistical significance. So if you're preparing for *Jeopardy!*, know your dates and study the most popular topics to give yourself the best advantage.

Discovering New Topics from Clues

In preparing to compete on *Jeopardy!*, a very important question is whether there are clues (or topics) from the early episodes that are as relevant as clues from later shows. Said another way, are the topics asked about on *Jeopardy!* changing over time, or are they stable? This type of question is also very important to organizations that deal with text because we know that fashion trends, political views, economic factors, and pop culture change over time and being able to identify new topics trending in future unforeseen data gives organizations the ability to detect these shifts. The baseline topics can be applied for discriminating what topics are continuing to be captured while allowing for new topics to emerge that are not accounted for by the existing topics. This model is ideal for yielding new topics that occur chronologically and can be scaled to account for new topics occurring at time $t+1, t+2, \ldots, t+N$.

Baseline topics are either manually assembled by the user through providing topic names, terms, roles, and weights or are automatically learned topics that have been modified subsequently. For the *Jeopardy!* topics, all have been automatically learned. Once baseline topics have been created, they can be applied to new data for identifying what is continuing to trend while allowing for new topics to be learned automatically.

Applying this to the J!-Archive data, the baseline data was taken from the years 1995 through 2000. The top five topics from those years are shown in Table 10.4.

These five topics were then applied to data from 2005 to 2010. Making the periods nonconsecutive ensured that a topic could not have appeared at the end of one period and then faded early in the next period. Holding the topics from the first period constant and also allowing new topics to be formed preserves the ability to identify these new topics and their relative size compared to the original topics identified in the first time period. The result of the analysis show that new topics are emerging. In Table 10.5 you can see how the popularity ranking of the topics changed. The new most popular topic was Women in History with questions like "Born in 1961, this famous woman was the daughter of the Eighth Earl of Spencer" (Princess Diana).

From the results in Table 10.5, you can see that topics do change over time but not drastically. From this analysis we find that more weight should be given to topics that are from more recent games than those from 20 years ago. By following this methodology, topic trending can be performed for a variety of types of sequentially ordered data. Then exploration, discovery, and monitoring can be performed to transform this stream of unstructured information into business value for your organization.

Contestant Analysis: Fantasy *Jeopardy!*

As a final look at the power of text analytics, the information of *Jeopardy!* clues will be combined with structured data to predict the success of *Jeopardy!* contestants. The contestants' previous performances on the show and the clues that they responded to are used to predict how the contestants would perform on questions from games in which

Table 10.4 Top Five Topics from 1995 to 2000

Topic	Common Terms	Number of Clues
Island Geography	Large	2,114
	Island	
	World	
	Group	
	Mile	
Music	Hit	1,817
	Song	
	Group	
	Hear	
	Sing	
Literature	Novel	1,738
	Author	
	Publish	
	Base	
	Book	
Screen	Play	1,538
	TV	
	Series	
	Actor	
	Movie	
Famous Firsts	First	1,468
	Woman	
	World	
	Book	
	Publish	

Table 10.5 Topic Popularity Ranking for Two Time Periods

Topic	1995–2000 Rank	2005–2010 Rank
Island Geography	1	2
Music	2	5
Literature	3	9
Screen	4	13
Famous Firsts	5	8

they did not participate. Ken Jennings participated in 75 games in his continuous winning streak in 2004. He correctly responded to 2,729 questions (91% correct) while incorrectly responding to 256. Additional data was included outside of Ken's winning streak, including data from the fifth round of the Tournament of Champions,[8] which aired on May 23, 24, and 25, 2005, and two days from the IBM Challenge, which aired February 15 and 16, 2011.

To predict if contestants will correctly respond to a clue they were never exposed to during the show, the questions they did answer, either correctly or incorrectly, must be analyzed. The clues that a contestant responded to were put into a training set. The clue text was then filtered, parsed, and clustered, and singular value decompositions were made in a number of dimensions. With the binary target variable of the contestants' responses and the SVDs from their training, many predictive modeling techniques (including all the ones discussed in Chapter 5) were used to build models with the objective to minimize the misclassification.

After building a model for Ken Jennings, Brad Rutter, and Jerome Vered (three of the players with the most longevity in the game's history), I could then predict their expected earnings for an arbitrary episode of the show that none of them participated in.

I was able to predict with very high accuracy whether the men would respond correctly or not to an arbitrary clue. Then using the questions from a show that aired when none of the contestants appeared, as shown in Table 10.6, I scored the questions using the model and calculated the expected earnings based on the probability of a correct response and then adjusted the earnings based on the percent-

Table 10.6 Projected Earnings from Three Contestants

Contestant	Projected Earnings		
	6/6/02	10/25/07	7/7/08
Ken Jennings	$27,619	$27,132	$27,384
Brad Rutter	$22,532	$24,602	$30,615
Jerome Vered	$14,061	$19,908	$14,122

---

[8] The Tournament of Champions is an invitation event for past winners to compete against each other

Table 10.7 Overall Response Profile

Contestant	Correct Responses	Incorrect Responses	Correct Response	Response Rate
Ken Jennings	2,723	256	91%	62%
Brad Rutter	524	50	91%	78%
Jerome Vered	402	40	91%	43%

age of questions the contestants responded to.[9] Table 10.7 shows the comparison of the three players with respect to the number of questions and their success at responding correctly.

It is interesting to see in Table 10.7 that these three successful contestants all had a 91% correct response rate but had such different response rates. While there is no way to know how any of these contestants would actually have performed on the show for a game they did not participate in, there are some comparisons that reinforce my projections. Ken Jennings's average daily winnings during his 74-game win streak was $33,727 and his average final Jeopardy! wager was $7,698.[10] If you take his average final Jeopardy! wager and add it to his projected earnings, you get a sum that is within 5% of his average payout.

While this example of comparing *Jeopardy!* contestants from different periods against each other likely will never become as popular as discussion of the greatest quarterback of all time, the ability to take text and combine it with structured data to get better predictive models is still relatively new for most organizations. I hope that this example has helped you begin to think how you can use text mining in your organization to improve your data-driven decisions and use of analytics.

---

[9] The expected earnings did not take into account daily doubles so for comparison assume that no one found the daily doubles.

[10] Ken's highest game was $75,000 and his lowest game was $8,799.

Success Stories of Putting It All Together

True genius resides in the capacity for evaluation of
uncertain, hazardous, and conflicting information.

—Winston Churchill

P arts One and Two explained the proper tools with which to manage data and the tools for analyzing it. Part Two also discussed the
techniques that give you the best opportunities to uncover new
information and confirm your hypotheses about your business. In this
part, I have compiled a collection of cases that illustrate companies that
have been able to use this information to find business value. In some
cases, this value has amounted to millions of dollars added or millions
of dollars saved, but in each case analytics were successfully applied to
well-stored and well-prepared data that improved the business.

I have worked with each of these companies to varying degrees. In
a few cases, I served in an advisory role or gave details about the software they were using to help them efficiently achieve their business
objective. In others, I was more involved and actually performed the
analysis myself to help prove out the business value.

These cases come from companies in different industries and coun-
ties. In most cases, they are large multinational corporations that faced
and overcame major challenges in using their data effectively. My
hope is that you can use these cases as a blueprint for applying process
and experience to your business challenge to make rapid headway and
achieve results. Taking raw data and turning that data into valuable information is a precious skill that is highly esteemed in the marketplace
and should be trained, cultivated, and acquired whenever possible.

QUALITIES OF SUCCESSFUL PROJECTS

All of the successful projects have a number of items in common. The
commonalities were not similar industries, or organizational structure, or even language. First among the common elements were an
executive sponsor who valued this information and appreciated that
analytics could be used to gain insight from data being collected.

The business value was easy to explain to people of all levels at the
company.

A commonality that I did not expect before I complied all of these cases is that the data was already being collected. I did not encounter a situation where an executive sponsor wanted the answer to a question that was not available from analyzing the existing data. This recognition brought me to appreciate that sometimes advantageous choices in the past pay dividends into the future.

CHAPTER 11

Case Study of a Large U.S.-Based Financial Services Company

The U.S. banking industry, because of government regulations and its utilization by almost all citizens, has by necessity lots of data. Some of the data is kept to comply with regulatory requirements, and some is kept to help the institution provide quality service and access to beneficial financial instruments to its customers. To sift efficiently and effectively through all the data being kept and distill useful information from that data poses a challenge for banks.

The bank under consideration serves millions and millions of customers. It frequently engages in marketing campaigns to offer both current and potential customers new relevant products and services. This case study is a marketing campaign to identify likely people to respond to an offer for a new credit card. This scenario is repeated frequently at this and many other banks and also applies to many other companies that offer products to customers. The ability to effectively predict which potential customers will respond to a marketing offer is very valuable for several reasons. The first is that it builds customer confidence by not sending junk mail or spam. The next reason is it allows the bank to reduce its expenses by not printing and mailing unwanted materials or hiring call center staff to make unwanted phone calls. The last reason is that getting customers signed up for the services they want generates revenue for the bank.

Credit cards generate revenue for banks through several methods. This revenue is categorized as two types: cardholder fees and vendor fees. Cardholder fees include annual fees, late fees, over-limit fees, interest paid fees, and so on. Vendor fees are transaction fees paid by vendors for each use of the card in exchange for guarantee of payment. As you would expect, there are significant costs associated with campaign marketing activities so being able to more accurately predict a potential customer's response to the credit card offer is very important. Better model accuracy leads to lower costs, better brand reputation, and improved customer loyalty. For this case study, the primary objective is better model accuracy.

The bank also had a second objective: improved operational processing efficiency and responsiveness. This bank has an IT infrastructure that is very common in the industry. It has several large enterprise data warehouses (EDWs) that store data about all current customers, past customers, and identified potential customers. The type of information stored in the EDWs ranges from customer account information, such as your mailing address or date of birth, to information provided by third parties, such as your credit score. There is also transactional information including each purchase you have made with a bank-issued credit card or call record for when you spoke to a customer service representative or used the automated system to pay your bill or check your account balance. The set of EDWs are, for this case, a set of massively parallel processing (MPP) databases.

TRADITIONAL MARKETING CAMPAIGN PROCESS

The marketing campaign follows a set of serialized steps that are well established and operationally defined. They are described next.

Gather the data. A campaign begins once a proposal is approved from the business executive. At that point a request is sent from the marketing department to its IT business partner. The request is to acquire data from the EDWs for all current and potential customers that adhere to certain criteria for the purpose of building a response model. The IT department gathers the data using several tools (most are Structured Query Language (SQL) based) as they extract the relevant information and aggregate it to the account or household level. Since marketing is done at a household level, information must be rolled up or aggregated to that level of detail.

At any given time, there are many credit card campaigns going. Since much of the same information about customers is needed in each campaign, it is operationally more efficient to create a standard base table for modeling on a regular interval—monthly in this case—so that many teams are able to use the same base table and then customize only the portion of data specific to a particular campaign. Having multiple teams use the same data provides for consistency, reduces the number of copies of the data and thus saves storage space, and creates an economy of scale for the creation of the base modeling table. The economy of scale comes from having one central group do the data preparation work once. Many model-building groups take advantage of the central data preparation instead of numerous different staff members doing essentially the same task for different marketing campaigns. The other economy of scale comes from the specialization that comes when you break up the data preparation from model building so that you do not require individuals to be experts in both domains. The consistency comes in through the treatment of the variables. One example is binning of continuous variables. Binning is a very common technique to simplify computations and to make interpretation easier. Age is a common variable that has high predictive power in likelihood to respond to certain marketing campaigns and also has special treatment for certain ages of potential clients.

Here is an example to further explain why binning variables can be a useful practice and consolidating that task leads to operational efficiency and better control:

The U.S. government in May of 2009 passed the Credit Card Accountability Responsibility and Disclosure Act of 2009, or Credit

CARD Act of 2009 for short. This act defines, and largely limits, the type of marketing activities that are permitted to people under 21 years of age. If the age variable were left as a continuous factor, it would require postprocessing to eliminate those potential customers from the model and at the same time introduce bias (because the people under 21 were used to fit the model but are not able to receive marketing offers). If the age variable is binned in this way—under 18, 18–20, 21–29, 30–34, and so on—we can simply filter prospects that fall into the ineligible bins.

After the IT department has completed its process of preparing the data, the modeling teams are notified.

Creating the model. In order to create a predictive model, you must identify the customers' attributes you know that help predict the outcome. The input data (containing the customer attributes or independent variables) will be a mix of interval, nominal, and binary variables. The number of customer attributes that will be considered initially to predict the binary response target of "respond to offer" or "no response" will be hundreds to sometimes thousands of variables. The modeler begins by reviewing the relationship of the response target and the customer attributes. This comparison will be done using correlation statistics and/or simple plots, such as histograms or bar charts. An investigation of missing values often is performed at this point and a plan put into place to address them (or a conscious choice to not address them).

Once the modeler has some initial assessment of the relationships between candidate variables and the target variable, the modeler will then split the data into mutually exclusive partitions. One partition will be used for building the model. This is often referred to as the training set. The other partition, the validation set, is for checking the generalized fit of the model. The validation set is used to protect against overfitting. Overfitting the model will lead to poor model generalization, a lower response rate from customers, and ultimately less revenue for the bank. After the data has been divided into partitions and initial exploration has been completed, the variable selection and model fitting begins in earnest. Building a predictive model is a highly iterative process with the goal being to get the simplest model (least number of customer attributes) that best predicts those who will respond to the offer without overfitting. The reasons this process is iterative are because many statistical and machine learning techniques can be used to fit a model, and each technique has a number of parameters that can be tuned in the model-building phase. There is no silver bullet technique that will always give the best model, although some techniques are better than others.

The final phase in this step is the assessment of all the candidate models to pick a best model. Many measures can be used to determine the "best" model. Some of these measures are averaged squared error (ASE), misclassification rate, and profit. It often happens that a technique will dominate the various measures, but situations exist where one modeling technique will appear best with one measure and another technique will appear best for another measure. Along the way, some candidate models are discarded, but almost always there are at least a few techniques that need to be evaluated in this final step. At this point, supervisory team members or managers are involved in the review process to make the final model selection.

Scoring the model. The marketing department is then given the model logic so that it can be applied to the entire potential customer table. Selecting a tool with integration between the modeling and the scoring steps can save the organization considerable time and money. With proper integration, the model logic can be applied to all customers in minutes; if the model logic has to be converted from one technology to another and then tested and verified, it can be weeks because of the manual involvement.

Rank your potential customers. The potential customers would then be ranked by their likelihood to respond or by the profitability they would bring. This ranking is as simple as creating a new column in the potential customer table. Once this column is populated with a customer's likelihood to respond or predicted profit, the table is then sorted in descending order so that the most likely respondents are on top.

Operationalize your campaign. The operational aspects of addressing, sending customized email, or placing outbound calls to potential customers does not begin until the budget for that campaign has been exhausted. A last step and best practice is to review the results of the marketing campaign and access how effective the model was in meeting its objectives.

The process just outlined has challenges when it is implemented in real-world situations. For example, during the steps of data assembly from the EDWs, model creation, and model application and scoring, the underlying customer data was changing. Customers were applying for new credit cards, missing car payments, changing their contact policies, moving to new states, and other possibilities from a near-limitless list of things that happen. These events that are external to the marketing campaign require human reconciliation, which is costly and slows down the process. The typical turnaround on a marketing campaign from the initial data pull to offers being sent to customers is a month.

The model lift, a metric to describe the predictive power compared to a random baseline, was between 1.5 and 2 at the second decile (20% mark). This means the selected final model was 1.5 to 2 times better than a random model when looking at the first fifth of the data. To put it another way, if you have 1000 potential prospects and 50 are going to respond to your campaign, if you take a 20% random sample, you would get, on average, 10 responders in the group of 200. After using the model to help you select who will be in the campaign, you expect to get 15 to 20 responders in the same 200 people.

The model lift in this case was restricted by the time window allowed for the modelers to work. As mentioned previously, the model-building process is very iterative, and modelers get better results as they have time to iterate through the model-building process. It is well known that the more time you give to building your model, the better the model will be.

HIGH-PERFORMANCE MARKETING SOLUTION

The financial institution adopted a big data computing appliance approach using a MPP database. This had two advantages.

1. It has a much larger aggregate memory and computational capacity than any single machine could provide. With more memory and computational power, the bank could use more

historical data and more candidate variables than previously, which allowed it to find patterns that were not discovered in the samples of the data it used previously.

2. It minimized data movement. With the decreased data movement and the additional computational power available, the bank was able to build the same models in minutes instead of many hours as it had been done before. One of the most dramatic improvements was for a model that had taken 19 hours to run now took 3 minutes to run. With this additional time, the modelers at the bank were able to try more statistical and machine learning techniques to search for a more effective model to predict who would respond to the campaign. They were also able to tune the models more. The use of additional techniques and greater refinement of the parameters resulted in a model with better lift—it was better at identifying those people who would respond to the marketing campaign.

VALUE PROPOSITION FOR CHANGE

The value proposition for this bank can be described in several ways: accuracy and precision, productivity for employees, more efficient processes, and increased revenue or return on investment.

The bank took advantage of the combination of the increased number of modeling techniques it could try, the increased time it had to tune each technique, and the increased data it could use for creating the model, and it was able to move the model lift from 1.6 to 2.5. This is a significant increase in model accuracy. Referring back to our 1000-customer example, now instead of finding 10 responders with no model or 16 with the traditional modeling approach, with this new high-performance appliance, the bank was able to identify 25 responders in the 200 people selected in the top 20%. This technology increased model accuracy.

With the decrease in model-building runtimes, the bank's analysts were able to complete their work in a shorter time, which allowed them to work on modeling marketing campaigns they otherwise would have not been able to do. The time-per-model-run went from one day to one hour; that translates into less staff or more models being produced without increasing staffing. This increased employee productivity.

Because of the reduced time to create the model, the amount of reconciliation and human intervention needed at the end of the campaign preparation phase was reduced, which had an additive effect of reducing the time to produce a marketing campaign and the human expense to create it. This made the process more efficient.

Because this process was more efficient, took less time, was more accurate, and took less staff, it is better in every measurable way. By computing the savings of staff time, the lifetime value of each acquired customer, and the improved brand reputation through better public perception about marketing efforts (i.e., people feel the bank sends less spam), the bank was able to quickly realize a positive return on investment measured in months.

CHAPTER **12**

Case Study of a Major Health Care Provider

The health care industry is seeing an increase in the data it has available and the expectation from customers and shareholders that this data be used to improve customer satisfaction, improve patient care, and return a higher value to shareholders.

The increase in data comes from several sources. The first is from electronic medical records. In years past, the information available to health care providers would be a claim form (either paper or electronic) that was processed to reimburse physicians for their services. Then prescription drugs were added so that some initial analysis could be made and help save patients from potentially harmful drug interactions. But in this era of electronic medical records, information far beyond the billing codes can be processed and analyzed. Physician notes, radiology reports, and transcribed phone calls to on-call nurse hotlines are all now potentially available. A major challenge to data of this type is that it is largely unstructured, which poses potentially significant challenges in productively using this data for improved decision making.

In fact, it is estimated that nearly 80% of all data is unstructured, and medical records can be some of the hardest to work with. Due to its own set of shorthand and abbreviations, extra care must be taken in organizing this information.

This case study is illustrative of the win-win opportunities that exist for both businesses and consumers. When businesses harness the data at their disposal and turn that into actionable information, customers get a better product—in this case better health benefits and proactive resolution of concerns—and businesses can reduce their expenses and increase their revenue, leading to substantially increased profits. This health care provider administers a large number of Medicare Advantage plans with many participants across the United States.

Medicare Advantage is a health insurance plan that is offered by private providers to add benefits, or provide an advantage, over the standard Medicare plan. Medicare is a standard health benefit package that covers older adults and those with disabilities since 1965. Medicare Advantage has more than 41 million participants, just over one in eight people living in the United States. The U.S. government pays the private provider a set monthly fee per member. Members may have a premium to pay out of pocket depending on the plan type and coverage they elect. Medicare Advantage has been an ongoing program since 1997 with a revision in 2003. Under the Patient Protection and Affordable Care Act of 2010 (or as it was referred to in the most recent U.S. presidential election, Obamacare), the Medicare Advantage plans have recently seen considerable change.

The changes made during the act of 2010 emphasized the quality of the plan and making data about quality more available and transparent to participants and the public at large. Each plan receives a star rating from one to five stars. One star is the lowest rating, and five stars is the best rating. A three-star plan is average. The Centers for Medicare and Medicaid Services (CMS), a government agency within the Health and Human Services Department, is responsible for assigning the ratings. The star ratings are aggregates of five different ratings systems: CAHPS (Consumer Assessment of Healthcare Providers and Systems), HEDIS (Healthcare Effectiveness Data and Information Set), HOS (Health Outcomes Survey), IRE (Independent Review Entity), and CMS. Brief explanations of some of the individual rating systems are included next.

CAHPS

This program is a multiyear initiative of the Agency for Healthcare Research and Quality to support and promote the assessment of consumers' experiences with health care. First launched in October 1995, it aims to address a range of health care services and meet the information needs of health care consumers, purchasers, health plans, providers, and policy makers. The goals of the CAHPS program are twofold:

1. Develop standardized patient surveys that can be used to compare results across sponsors and over time.
2. Generate tools and resources that sponsors can use to produce understandable and usable comparative information for both consumers and health care providers.

The various CAHPS surveys ask consumers and patients to report on and evaluate their experiences with health care. These surveys cover topics that are important to consumers and focus on aspects of quality that consumers are best qualified to assess, such as the communication skills of providers and ease of access to health care services.

HEDIS

HEDIS consists of 80 measures across five domains of care. HEDIS measures address a broad range of important health issues. Among them are the following:

- Asthma medication use
- Persistence of beta-blocker treatment after a heart attack
- Controlling high blood pressure
- Comprehensive diabetes care
- Breast cancer screening
- Antidepressant medication management
- Childhood and adolescent immunization status
- Childhood and adult weight/body mass index assessment

HEDIS is designed to provide purchasers and consumers with the information they need to reliably compare the performance of health care plans.

HOS

The goal of the Medicare HOS program is to gather valid and reliable health status data in Medicare-managed care for use in quality improvement activities, plan accountability, public reporting, and improving health. Managed care plans with Medicare Advantage contracts must participate.

IRE

IRE is an appeals process for those who feel they have been unfairly treated or denied services owed them under their plan benefits.

In using these assessment instruments, the Medicare health plans are rated in five different categories

1. Stay healthy: screenings, test, and vaccines
2. Managing chronic conditions
3. Member experience with the health plan
4. Member complaints, problems getting services, and improvement in the health plan's performance
5. Health plan customer service

As you can see, members' feelings about their health plans are very important components to the star rating. The star rating is also critical to reimbursement of the plan for services it provides. Here is how the process works.

For each county in the United States, a benchmark value is established for the Medicaid and Medicare monthly cost of care. This benchmark varies from county to county due to a number of factors. Medicare Advantage plans then bid on the cost to provide coverage for Medicare parts A and B benefits (the original coverage) for the eligible participants of that county. If the bid amount is under the benchmark value (which it usually is), then the plan providers receive a percentage of the difference between the bid price and the benchmark value back from the county in the form of a rebate. This provides incentives to the plans to provide the required standard of care at the lowest price—all plans are required to cover all the tenants of Medicare part A and B. The rebate must be used to provide extra benefits to the enrollee.

The rebate is the first place that the star rating affects revenue. The rebate amount a plan receives is modified by the star rating, where five-star plans receive a larger rebate than a three- or four-star plan with the same bid. Here is an example: If the benchmark for Mesa County, Colorado, is $300 per month and plan XYZ bids $280, it receives 67% of the difference back in a rebate ($300 − $280)×.67 = $13.40 per participant. This rebate is adjusted based on the star rating of plan XYZ. If it is a five-star plan, then the rebate is 73% (or a rebate of $14.60) instead of $13.60. In addition to increasing the rate of the rebate reimbursement, the benchmark value is adjusted so the adjusted benchmark for Mesa County for a five-star plan is $315 ($300×1.05), which results in a total rebate of $25.55. The difference between the original rebate and the adjusted rebate is termed the bonus. For this example, plan XZY will receive a bonus of $12.15 per member. Here, having a five-star plan almost doubled the profit per member as compared to a three-star plan.

The bonus is paid for with funds designated in the Health Reform Law and also from funds established for a demonstration period. These two sources of funding total about $3.1 billion in bonus allocation for 2012.

The reward for having a five-star plan increases during the period of 2012 to 2014 as the bonus percentage increases in each year as this new quality component is phased in. In addition to additional revenue, the CMS is further adding emphasis on customer satisfaction by allowing customers to move from their current plan, if it is rated less than five stars, to a five-star plan at any time. Before, customers normally could change plans only during the annual open season.

This health care provider has plans rated above average. Given the potential revenue that could be generated from having a five-star plan, it made good business sense to invest in using the unstructured data it was already storing to help determine customer satisfaction and intervene as needed. The early investment in producing five-star plans is a virtuous cycle that can lead to billions of dollars in additional revenue over the course of several years.

This company already has a significant investment in analytical talent and a number of predictive models to help inform decision makers, but there was a wealth of unstructured data, most in the form of text, which was not being used. This was seen as a great opportunity to use the textual information recorded by the customer support representatives (CSRs—the operators who answer the phone when customers call with questions) to aid in identifying those customers who were unhappy or needed some additional assistance in resolving their issues or problems.

All parties can be proud of their success in addressing this problem. I have aging family members who participate in Medicare Advantage, and I want them to be happy with their health care experience. The company wants to have happy participants because it engenders goodwill, improves customer loyalty, and reduces the overhead costs to administer the plan (less correspondence to send and less call center staff, etc.), which in turn allows the company to offer better benefits at the same rate or equivalent benefits at a lower rate. The third reason is that the reimbursement rate from the U.S. government is determined in part by the customer satisfaction rating that each plan gets.

Almost every plan member is satisfied with this plan provider, so identifying dissatisfied customers is difficult because they are rare (which was discussed in Chapter 4) but one that is crucial as the plan administrator wants all plan members to be pleased with their coverage.

More satisfied patients stay with their current plan. Satisfied patients encourage primary care and specialist physicians to accept plan terms.

The business challenge faced was that in the current environment, only a small portion of the records could be modeled. A great source of information—the transcripts of phone calls with the call center—was not available in the modeling process.

The business problem was to improve customer satisfaction. To do this, more records had to be used to improve model accuracy and more attributes, namely CSR notes taken during a call, needed to be considered in the modeling process. The implemented solution was an MPP database that was used as a distributed in-memory modeling appliance. The training data set was 169 million records with each record being about

5 kilobytes in length. This length consisted of hundreds of fields but also several large text fields. The process followed five steps:

1. **Gather the data.** This consists of federating data from several enterprise data warehouse (EDW) systems. In addition to the EDW, there is data from transactional systems, MS Access databases, Excel spreadsheets, flat files, and several other sources. This represents some of the true issues with solving data mining problems. This pain point is easier than it would have been in previous attempts because of the ample storage space provided by the MPP database and the parallelism in the loads. For this proof of concept, the data used is all of the relevant structured data that could be gathered and the text fields that contain the CSR notes from call centers throughout the country. The IT department in conjunction with analytical staff performs this function of gathering data together for analysis.

2. **Load the data**. With a single table containing all the modeling features created, that table was loaded in and distributed into the MPP database. The size of the data file was about 800 gigabytes. Using the distributed loading capabilities, the table loaded in about 20 minutes. This is a significant improvement over previous attempts using different technology.

3. **Model the data**. There are a number of reasons that customers might call the health care administrator: billing issues, access to health care—the doctor they want to see is out of network or none of the in-network providers have timely appointments. Customers also call because of medication issues—the medication that their doctor prescribed is not available in a nonformulary (non–name brand, such as statin versus Lipitor®). For each of the general reasons that customers call, models need to be created. Each class of model might have several subcategories that have models associated with them. The predictive models have some shared attributes but unique attributes as well.

   To make use of the text data, a singular value decomposition (SVD) is then performed. For those unfamiliar with SVDs, they are a factorization of a matrix analog to an eigenvalue or principal component. The SVDs combined with the structured variables from the EDW were used to create models to predict the likelihood that a customer would be dissatisfied. The models do not decay very quickly compared to models in other industries, and they often remain valid for many months. The biggest reason models decay is due to changes in plan benefits. Each year participants have an open season during which they can switch plans. Plan administrators must notify customers of any plan changes in advance of the open season so that customers can make an informed choice. The models are sensitive to these plan changes, and significant effort is spent to identify similar situations in the historical data and estimate the correlation and potential impact. The reduced time required to build models has led to a more tactical approach to model building, because the decay point of the model is known in advance and the likely drivers are also known. The analytics team is able prepare for the event and then take early information from the first few days of customer calls to build a relevant model. This avoids the lengthy process of determining surrogates in the historical data and then running simulations to predict customer behavior. The team is able to monitor the response and then make adjustments. This leads to better models and a more efficient use of the modeling team's time.

The health care provider remarked during this process that without this high-performance appliance, it would have never attempted to model a problem of this size; it just would not have been feasible. A number of modeling techniques mainly in the family of logistic regression and neural networks were considered, and multiple iterations to each were attempted to get the highest-quality model. These iterations, because they were running in a distributed in-memory appliance, were done in minutes where days would have been required previously. This reduction in time for building each model iteration allowed for many more iterations of each model and the opportunity to consider additional modeling techniques. This combination of considering more techniques and having more chances to refine each technique will always lead to better models.

4. **Score the models.** With the models built, each call record is scored by each model to create a probability score for a customer being dissatisfied. The patient's scores from each model are then sorted, summed, and ranked. The summing is done because a customer may be scored as dissatisfied by multiple models, and that aggregate score is relevant.

5. **Apply to the business.** Two of the most powerful features that have taken root in this organization are (1) the predictive power of the models and their ability to identify situations where intervention is warranted and (2) the ability to group search terms to present all the relevant data to the business user. For example, there are more than 20 different spellings for the term "grievance" (I spelled it wrong in several drafts myself) in the CSR notes. Historically, business users would have to repeat their search multiple times for each variation (and hope that they guessed them all). Then business users would be required to make aggregate graphs based on what they saw or try to decide which spelling best approximated what they saw for the entire population. With this high-performance appliance, search terms can be collapsed and managed at a global level to give users the complete information they need.

The high-performance appliance is used primarily to provide insight into the massive amount of data that this health care provider is responsible for and also to test business analysts' hypotheses on why certain situations are occurring with customers.

This proof of concept was so successful that funding was immediately secured to make the project permanent. The end goal is to have every customer call transcribed and every customer touch point scored. Additionally each call would be scored for sentiment and classified into categories based on the contents of the call. All of this is possible now when it was only wishful thinking a few years ago.

This predictive modeling process to predict patient satisfaction has been able to help the health care provider better focus its efforts on those patients who need additional help. This increased effort and attention ensures patients better medical care and hopefully improved medical outcomes. It also allows the health care provider to spend human capital resources where they are needed most and reduce costs while returning a better value product for customers and higher earnings for shareholders. In the future, this single program has the ability to affect millions and millions of dollars in profit annually through achieving and maintaining a five-star rating.

CHAPTER **13**

Case Study of a Technology Manufacturer

The manufacturing line is a place where granular analysis and big data come together. Being able to determine quickly if a device is functioning properly and isolate the defective part, misaligned machine, or ill-behaving process is critical to the bottom line. There were hundreds of millions of TVs, cell phones, tablet computers, and other electronic devices produced last year, and the projections point to continued increases for the next several years.

FINDING DEFECTIVE DEVICES

To visit the manufacturing facility of the latest and greatest electronic manufacturers is to almost enter a different world. People wearing what looks like space suits, robots moving in perfect synchronization, all as machines roar and product moves through the many steps from raw material to parts and then finally to an inspected flawless finished product.

When a failure is detected in the manufacturing process, there is an immediate need to identify the source of the problem, its potential size, and how to correct it. Doing this requires analyzing thousands of potential variables and millions to even billions of data points. This data, in addition to being very large in size, is also very time critical. There is a finite window of time after a problem is discovered to stop the defective batch of product from leaving the factory and then also to address the root cause before more time and material are wasted. This efficient treatment of defective product also helps to maintain good brand reputation, worker morale, and a better bottom line.

HOW THEY REDUCED COST

The typical path of resolution for this type of modeling for this customer is outlined in the next six steps.

1. The first step is the inspection process for the product. Each product has a specified inspection process that is required to ensure quality control guidelines are met and the product is free from defects. For example, determining if a batch of silicon wafers meets quality control guidelines is different from determining quality control acceptance for a computer monitor. In the case of the wafer, the result is essentially a binary state: The wafer works or it does not. If it does not work, it is useless scrap because there is not a mechanism to repair the wafer. In the case of the computer monitor, it could be that there is a dead pixel, or a warped assembly, or discoloration in the plastic, or dozens of other reasons the monitor does not pass quality control guidelines. Some of these product defects can be remediated by repeating the assembly process or swapping out a defective part; others cannot be remediated, and the monitor must be written off as waste. In these complex devices, humans are still much better at visual inspection to determine defects in the display (for more details see the Neural Networks section in Chapter 5) than teaching a computer to see. The human eye is very developed at seeing patterns and noticing anomalies. In this manufacturing environment, the human quality control

team members can find more reasons for rejection than the computer system by an order of magnitude.

If a product batch does not meet the quality control threshold, then an investigation is initiated. Because the investigation slows or stops the ability to manufacture additional items, an investigation is not done on a random basis but only after a batch of product has failed quality control inspection. This investigation is expensive in terms of time, quantity, and disruption, but it is essential to prevent the assembly of faulty products.

2. Once a batch of wafers, for example, has failed quality control, an extract of data from the enterprise data warehouse (EDW) is requested. This data is sensor data over the last few days from a number of different source systems. Some of the data is stored in traditional massively parallel process (MPP) databases; other data is stored in Hadoop and still other in neither Hadoop nor MPP databases. This is a complex process that involves joining a number of tables stored in a relational schema of third normal form and denormalizing them to a rectangular data table along with matching them to MPP tables. The process to manufacture a single wafer can include several thousand steps and result in more than 20,000 data points along the assembly line process. When this data is transformed and combined with millions and millions of wafers manufactured every day, you have truly big data. The assembled rectangular data table is of a size that would defy the laws of physics to move for processing in the allotted time window of a few hours.

3. The data is then clustered. With such wide data (more than 10,000 columns) it is clear that not all will be responsible for the defects. The columns can be removed and clustered based on several criteria. The first is if the column is unary, or only has one value. With only one reading, the column holds no useful information in determining the source of the defects. The second is multicollinearity. Multicollinearity is a statistical concept for when two or more input variables, the measurements from the sensors in this case, are very highly correlated. Multicollinearity does not affect the final predictive power of the model, but it does needlessly increase the computational cost

of building the model because the model considers more terms than it really needs. Multicollinearity can lead to parameter estimates that are highly influenced by other input variables and thus are less reliable. This clustering step removes the useless variables and those that do not add additional predictive power because of their relationship to other input variables.

4. An equipment path analysis is now performed to try to identify the potential source of the problem. This analysis can be done using several techniques, but decision trees are often a popular choice for their high interpretability and simple assumptions. The problem historically has been the difficulty of using the needed volume of data in the required time window.

   Decision trees at a basic level attempt to split a set of data into the two purest groups by evaluating all the candidate variables and all the candidate split points. The calculation of the best split must be communicated, summarized, and then broadcast (in the case of a distributed environment) before the next split point can be determined. Because of this communication after each step, additional care in constructing efficient techniques to build decision trees is required in a parallel and distributed environment.

   After the best split is found, it must be evaluated to see if the split adds to the overall explanatory power of the tree. At some point in building almost every decision tree, the algorithm reaches a point that additional splits do not improve the results but needlessly complicate the tree model. This falls under the principle of parsimony. Parsimony is a principle that if two models (decision trees in this case) have equal explanatory or predictive power, then the simpler model is better. If the equipment path analysis yields suspect equipment, it is investigated. Historically, the decision tree has proven to be very effective at uncovering the systemic failure—a machine that is out of alignment or that has an inaccurate thermometer. It does not deal well with detecting interaction causes of defects. These are often termed random events because they are not attributable to a single cause and therefore cannot be easily diagnosed and fixed. An example of this might be that in step 341, a particle of dust interfered with encoding for item 123. That failed encoding caused a delay for item 113 on step 297, which resulted in an excess heat registered to sector A4 of the wafer. Because of the excess heat in sector A4, the chemical bath in step 632 did not adhere fully, which then caused a . . . (you get the idea). This type of complex reaction is not visible using decision trees. So other techniques specific to time series data—functional dimension analysis (FDA) or symbolic aggregate approximation (SAX) (see Chapter 8 for more details)—are being evaluated. This should remind us that even though dramatic improvements were achieved, there is still more research and work to be done to improve the process.

5. A root cause analysis is also performed. This is to identify the problem in procedure or process that leads to the error and the least common set of variables that need to be assessed to prevent the problem. With all the measurements, attributes, and metadata, taking every data artifact into account is time consuming and impractical. The least common or vital few analyses are done using a variable importance measure to determine what additional check can be added to prevent a repeat of this failure.

6. The results from both steps 3 and 4 are sorted, ranked, and analyzed for frequency. After this information is summarized, a report is issued with detailed timeline, problem, recommendations, and next steps.

In this case, the customer used the distributed file system of Hadoop along with in-memory computational methods to solve the problem within the business parameters. This process had been developed, refined, and improved over several years, but until the adoption of the latest distributed in-memory analytical techniques, a problem of this size was considered infeasible. After adopting this new infrastructure, the time to compute a correlation matrix of the needed size went from hours down to just a few minutes, and similar improvements were seen in the other analysis steps of an investigation. The customers are very pleased with the opportunity they now have to gain competitive advantage in high-tech manufacturing and further improve their process and their position in the market.

CHAPTER **14**

Case Study of Online Brand Management

I n this modern information age, business success is closely tied to your success on the Internet. This is especially true of manufacturers. On-line brand management is a challenging, fast-paced environment where ideas or perceptions that once took weeks can evolve in hours. The popular microblogging site Twitter reported in the fall of 2012 that it was now seeing 500 million tweets per day on the site. A quick search for this large company revealed thousands of tweets from their customers. With each five-second refresh, more than 20 new tweets would arrive almost around the clock. It is impossible for any human or any department of humans to keep up with all the customer comments about a company from just this one microblogging service. Now add up-dates from other popular social media sites like Facebook, LinkedIn, and others, and staying on top of consumers' thoughts on your product can appear to be an impossible task. The amount of information that must be processed to keep an accurate view of the brand's value and then be prepared to promote, defend, or anticipate changes in the brand can seem to be a daunting task.

A number of analytical techniques can be used to help tame this task. Here we will talk about Twitter, but these six techniques could be used for almost any human-generated feed of data.

1. Identify the language in which the user is commenting. Language detection is an important first step because it can help determine the size and scope of the issue or praise. By and large, Twitter users only use the site in one language with a few using two (almost always their mother tongue plus English). Identifying the language also helps to identify a location if the GPS locations are not available. (In my experience, this is of minor benefit since most tweets are made from smartphones, which include the location in their metadata.)

2. Look for sentiment. Sentiment analysis is a fantastic tool in managing a brand because it helps you focus in on those customers who are unhappy, the aspects of the product that cause the most problems, or those users who can be of help as advocates for your brand. The true power of sentiment analysis is that it not only informs you how customers feel about your product but it tells you how strongly they feel it. It also sheds light on if they feel this particular way about the entire product or just some aspects of the product. For example, consider an LCD TV display. This is a complex product with many individual features to like or dislike in addition to an overall sentiment. By first identifying the language, we can see that there are a higher-than-normal set of negative posts from Brazil, which might lead to an investigation of the translation quality of the user's manual or it might point out a product flaw that when the TV is left on for a large number of hours (like during the World Cup), the color saturation changes and it is harder to discern details in the content.

3. Categorize the content. There is some debate that I think boils down to personal preference about doing sentiment analysis before content categorization or vice versa. My personal preference for this order is that it allows me to use sentiment as a

filter for the most emergent issues, upset customers, and then categorize those feedback items.

4. Apply business rules to the situation. Once we have identified the sentiment of particular users and the categories that trouble or please them, we must now use the established business process for resolving their concern or leveraging the positive feedback in future activities. If current business processes do not include details on how to react in these types of situations, then those business processes will need to be established, but that is a separate discussion that will not be dealt with in this book.

An example of a standard business process for positive feedback is to retweet or like the comment so that users following you will see the positive comment and hopefully increase their brand loyalty and think more positively about your brand. In the case of negative comments, the options might be to send a private message to the customer, send them a list of the nearest retail stores so that they may exchange the product, or send a link to the frequently asked question (FAQ) page where this issue is addressed. The action does not need to be grand, but to be effective, it should be targeted to the customer's specific issue and it should be promptly after the complaint is registered. If this is done successfully, you will secure a more faithful following from this user, and the user is likely to influence those in their network of influence toward more positive sentiment about the brand.

5. Create models that can be used as a feedback loop. With the details that have been provided by the user, we can join that information with the structured data that already exists and create models that solve a number of useful purposes. We can incorporate positive feedback into updated sales forecasts and as triggers to suppliers for more parts. Negative feedback can be studied for product quality and issues with manufacturing processes or customer service training or usability design. As is often the case, in this step we can learn more from our critics than our advocates. While no one wants negative feedback, it is often the best source for product improvement.

6. Monitor the process. Once this process of identifying sentiment and moving comments into categories and following business rules for dealing with the feedback are in place, there are opportunities for continual improvement in this area just like any other. Key metrics for this area are the number of communications issued, average time to respond, and number of escalated concerns. It is also a worthwhile endeavor to look for correlation of your brand success and your online efforts. I doubt a causal link can be established in most cases, but showing efficacy in your efforts is the best way to keep funding and show the additional value your work brings to the company.

During this case study the focus is on the things that you can do to monitor your brand and product portfolio. The same ideas can be employed in trying to gain market share from your competitors. There are few times people are more willing to change habits (using a particular brand is a habit) than at the point directly after they have just expressed frustration with that habit. Your mileage will vary on the point depending on the goods or services your brand sells. Services are usually easier to displace than durable goods. But always being on the lookout for opportunities to take market share from competitors is a tried and true way for business to thrive.

CHAPTER 15

Case Study of Mobile Application Recommendations

With the rapid growth of smartphones over the past five years, a new market for smartphone applications has emerged and with it stiff competition for mind share. All vendors in this space desire the ability to make recommendations on the applications (apps) that users will like. The goal is to ensure that recommendations are not seen as spam (unwanted solicitations) but instead as great advice, thus moving from simply suggesting content to a highly prized role as a trusted advisor. The business problem in this case is very straightforward: Given the apps users have on their mobile phones, what apps are they likely to use? This problem poses several challenges, the first being the size of the data. With hundreds of millions of cell phone users and each one being almost unique in app purchases, finding good recommendations is difficult. The other issue is the level of detail about the apps. For this business challenge, the data was a set of binary variables. The binary state could be defined a number of different ways: Did they have the application installed? Had they ever used the application? Had the application been used in the last time period?

Table 15.1 Sparse Customer and Item Data Sheet

Customer	Item1	Item2	Item3	Item4. . .	ItemN
Customer1	1				1
Customer2			1		
Customer3				1	
Customer4. . .	1				
CustomerN		1			

Regardless of how you frame the problem, the output is a probability to purchase the app (the purchase price may be free) based on a set of binary input variables.

This problem is divided up into several stages, each requiring different skill sets. The first stage is data collection and aggregation. Traditional predictive modeling through data mining generally requires that input data be rectangular, and missing values pose severe problems for some algorithms. In this case, having a list of potential applications to recommend and all possible apps that could have been purchased as variables and all the customers as rows in the data (see Table 15.1) creates a very sparse data set. (There are lots of missing values.) Normally imputation would be an approach to deal with these missing values, but because the data is so sparse and the variables are binary, imputation is very difficult without creating bias and skewing results. This high level of missing values makes neural networks and logistic regression poor techniques for this type of problem. Decision trees can better handle missing values, but they tend to be unstable. The techniques of factorization machines or stochastic gradient descent generally behave better for these types of problems.

The second problem is data size. Because making recommendations while considering only a subset of the data is suboptimal, the quality of the recommendations is called into question. Therefore, sufficient computing hardware, especially main memory, must be allocated for the problem size along with software that is designed to perform in a parallel and distributed environment. The parallel nature allows all the CPU cores on the machine to be utilized, and the distribution property allows for multiple machines to work together solving the problem. This distributed nature also allows for expansion of your hardware as the problem size increases—this often happens after a successful implementation: New, larger problems emerge that, if they can be solved, will provide additional business value and are therefore very desirable.

The parallel and distributed design of the software also allows for a critical component: speed. It is not useful to solve a problem in a day if the answer is needed in a few seconds (what most people are willing to wait) and the answer cannot be precomputed. This problem is often overcome by doing offline training. The recommendation model is trained and refined using historical data and then deployed so that new events—a user coming to an app store, for example—is scored and apps are recommended. This pattern of offline training and model scoring solves the problem of quick recommendation but introduces the concern about the useful life of a model, or model decay. Having the ability to quickly train, deploy, and retrain is the ideal situation for recommendations that need to be near real time or faster. Alternatively, a service-based architecture could be used where the model is trained and then held in memory. When a recommendation is needed, an application program interface(API) is employed with the new record, and a recommendation is made using a content-based filtering or collaborative filtering method. These methods produce a small subset of the entire collection of apps available in the virtual store based on criteria and then update the overall table so that a future recommendation request will use all available information.

For this case study there were about 200 apps to be considered. The first step was to look for clusters that would help reduce the problem space. This clustering reduced the number of input variables from 200 down to a few dozen. After the clustering was completed, the cluster variables were added to the list of potential input variables. Other techniques included singular value decomposition, and principal component analysis to find relationships between apps. After the enrichment of the data with the additional features were created, variable selection techniques, both supervised and unsupervised, were used to eliminate variables that did not provide useful information. This was followed by multiple iterations of different tree models. The trees were boosted and ensembles were created in a variety of ways to produce powerful and stable models. The models were evaluated against a holdout sample that had been partitioned earlier—not randomly, as is typical, but by a time window. To randomly sample would have biased the recommendations because users were in both training and validation data, but with a time partition the model could be tested under real-world conditions, because once the model is developed and deployed, it must be updated with an active learning paradigm or retrained before excessive decay.

CHAPTER 16

Case Study of a High-Tech Product Manufacturer

Semiconductor wafer fabrication is very competitive. Companies compete on cost, quality, and delivery time to market. In the age of digital information, a large amount of data (e.g., process data, equipment data, and lots of historical data) has been automatically or semiautomatically collected, recorded, and accumulated for monitoring the process, diagnosing faults, and managing the manufacturing process. Decision makers may potentially use the information buried in the raw data to assist their decisions through data mining for possibly identifying the specific patterns of the data.

However, in the high-tech industry of semiconductor manufacturing, many factors that are interrelated affect the yield of fabricated wafers. Engineers who rely on specific domain knowledge cannot find possible root causes of defects rapidly and effectively. (See Figure 16.1.)

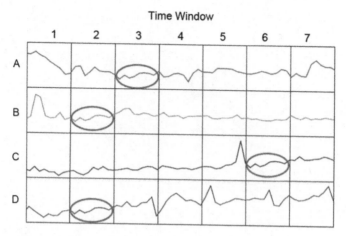

Figure 16.1 Time Series Similarity

In addition, when conducting similarity analysis for the time series data, the company also needs to identify and report separately the similarity according to the definable time windows; users are allowed to adjust and define these time windows when necessary. For example, in Figure 16.1, the similarity of time window 1, 5, 6 in time series A has a stronger similarity pattern than the others. Companies can decompose these time series similarities in different time windows for different machines.

HANDLING THE MISSING DATA

The collected semiconductor data often include missing and inconsistent data. Depending on the sources of the data, some of the yields in some processes are captured and measured only by sampling (for particular LOT ID). And some of the yields measured with particular LOTs which will be combined or split to other LOTs in the manufacturing processes.

Data preprocessing is required to improve the quality of the data and facilitate efficient data mining tasks. In particular, missing values are replaced or deleted; and in addition to some statistical way of missing data imputation, business rules are also adopted for handling the missing data. Some of the new variables combining machine number with date are generated.

The causal relationships between the machines of specific processes and the yield rate are examined and investigated by engineers. Different statistical methods are used to identify possible root causes (e.g., the specific machine where the failure occured). Semiconductor companies have been using decision trees to identify the root causes of the equipment path and other vital variables. By running the >2000 times including >5million devices data, the target variable is the equipment condition (good or not good), based on the equipment path (e.g., equipment ID, Step ID. . .).

In addition to the decision tree models for root cause analysis, the company has been exploring and validating different techniques for identification of root causes, including partial least square regression and gradient boosting. In the latest proof of concept, it requested consideration of the time dimension; the time series similarity matrix was used to investigate the pattern of processes (and machines) that leads to low yields. Clustering to automatically choose the best number of cluster groups can be done using cubic clustering criterion to estimate the number of clusters using Ward's minimum variance method, k-means, or other methods based on minimizing the within-cluster sum of squares.

Requirements focused on analyzing/processing "events in motion" for the machine/equipment-processed data. Continuous queries were made on data in motion (with incrementally updated results) and with the high volumes (more than 100,000 events/sec) stream processing was used to identify events via the time series similarity or "kernel library" events.

APPLICATION BEYOND MANUFACTURING

After successful results are realized in the manufacturing division for the company, methods and techniques will be rolled out to other parts of the company to allow them to take advantage of the big data analytic architecture. Some examples of planned projects are:

- Usage pattern analysis with log data from manufactured electronic devices

- Setup strategy in business to consumer device with big data
- Social media analysis
- Brand reputation
- Monitoring new trends in technology
- Call center performance
- Retail market quality
- Claim risk monitoring

CHAPTER 17

Looking to the Future

A s I look down the road to where I see big data, data mining, and machine learning in the future, I see many opportunities and some serious challenges. The biggest challenge that will need to be addressed is the balance between data privacy and reproducible research. I was asked to address this topic in a question-and-answer session during an invited talk at the Joint Statistical Meeting for the American Statistical Society in 2013. It is a difficult topic with no clear path forward. How we balance user privacy and reproducible research results is a decision that will impact all of us both as consumers and also as data users. It requires us as a society to define what our right to privacy actually includes. This balance of competing interests includes questions of legality as well as technology. Regardless of the outcome, there will be significant impacts on organizations in these ways: to comply with research standards, adhere to legislation, and fund enforcement of the laws.

REPRODUCIBLE RESEARCH

As my fourth-grade daughter can repeat from memory, the scientific method is: formulate a hypothesis, then test your hypothesis through an experiment, and finally analyze your results to determine if you can reject the hypothesis. A key outcome of a scientifically performed study is the reproducibility of the results. Unfortunately, this basic expectation has become increasingly rare. *The Economist* in October 2013 detailed the difficulty in getting reproducible results and suggests explanations for why it has become so hard to reproduce research results. One example cited that less than half of 238 biomedical papers published in 84 different journals could be reproduced. In another study, Amgen, a U.S. drug company, tried to replicate 53 landmark studies in the science of cancer; it was able to reproduce just 6. The U.S. government and many other developed nations around the world spend a significant amount of money to fund research to advance science in a number of disciplines. For example, the National Institutes of Health, which is part of the U.S. Department of Health and Human Services, spent over $25 billion in research funding in fiscal year 2012. What is our return on investment if some high percentage of that research is not actually advancing the various fields of study?

Tighter controls and accountability need to be put into place so that people and organizations are held accountable for their published research findings so that advances in areas of public good can build on top of a firm foundation, not quicksand.

PRIVACY WITH PUBLIC DATA SETS

The ability to identify people's behavior even before they might be aware of it does leave me with mixed emotion. Consider the story that *The New York Times Magazine* did on Target and its success in identifying women who are pregnant in order to take advantage of the opportunity to change purchasing habits. On one hand, I am proud to be part of a group that is advancing science and practice to the point that machines can detect patterns and positively identify these otherwise unobservable traits. On the other hand, I value my privacy and I am cautious about the information I volunteer to organizations, fearing that it will be shared with others I did not authorize. I look forward to the day when junk mail is no longer junk but exactly the ads I wanted. That day has certainly not yet arrived.

Arvind Narayanan is an associate professor in the Department of Computer Science at Princeton University. In a paper written in 2008, he outlined two strategies for taking data sets that contain microdata and combining that data with publicly available data to deanonymize a large data set.[1] In his example he uses the Netflix Prize data set, but the same could be done for a data set with DNA sequencing of a cancer drug study or any other large data set.

The first strategy is to match a few known items about a particular individual with the anonymous data. With this match, the entire set of attributes about the individual is revealed. By matching the ratings made on the publicly available IMDB ratings Web site and the Netflix data, individuals could be identified. Once a user was identified by matching between the two sources, the Netflix data revealed their full viewing history. Now you might be familiar with the Netflix Prize and think: Netflix only used a sample of the records, so how can you be sure you have the right person? When the information was matched, it produced a result that was 28 standard deviations away from the mean compared to no more than 2 standard deviations for every other customer.

Another interesting finding is that it required relatively little information about the movies watched to accurately identify an individual. This has to do with the sparse nature of the data; people watch relatively few movies compared to the size of the database. It turned out that knowing just six movies that a person watched allowed for a 99% match rate when the date of viewing was known within 14 days. This is data that could be easily overheard in the corporate lunchroom.

These research findings show how little thought most people have given to the privacy concerns in the big data era. It illustrates the point that additional information and computing power make it possible to deanonymize large data sets just like playing Sudoku, where there are a few known elements to start and through reason and deduction

---

[1] Microdata is information about specific people. Often it does not include unique identifiers but purchases, health histories, or viewing preferences.

more cell values can be identified, which in turn helps to identify even more cell values until all the cell values are known.

Contrast this lack of reproducible results with the danger of releasing large sets of big data that contain personal information. This will be a lively debate and will reduce the amount of crowd-sourced research and scientific advancement that can take place.

THE INTERNET OF THINGS

The idea of the Internet of Things was first presented by Kevin Ashton in 1999. Kevin Ashton, co-founder and executive director of the Auto-ID Center, is credited with coining the term the "Internet of Things." Ashton said he first used the term in a presentation in 1999 he made to Procter & Gamble on how to link the company's RFID supply chain technology to the Internet. Ashton was a marketer for Procter & Gamble (P&G) in the cosmetics area and was very frustrated that each time he surveyed products in stores, a number of items were out of stock. After many presentations to management at P&G, he was appointed to MIT as the executive director of the Auto-ID Center. The center was given $20 million in funding to reduce the cost of radio-frequency identification (RFID) tags. The funding came from many of the major retail brands, including Coke, Home Depot, Wal-Mart, Kraft, P&G, and so on. With reduced costs of RFID and by creating a situation where suppliers were required to use RFID for every pallet and shipment, machines were beginning to generate data that was sent to other machines (M2M communication). This idea that machines talk to machines without human involvement has also contributed to the occurrence of the big data era. The power of the RFID tag is to always know where a shipment is located. This reduces lost product due to theft, spoilage of perishable products like produce, and automated inventory replenishment systems. The power of RFID tagging is that retailers can now make truly personalized offers based on the items you have in your cart while you are still shopping.

As the Internet of Things continues to develop and mature, data volumes will continue to proliferate and more and more machines will be talking to one another on our behalf. Data generated by humans will fall to a small percentage in the next ten years. Capturing the relevant machine data and using it effectively in your organization will provide the biggest competitive advantage in the data mining space over the coming decade.

In the next ten years, the number of smart meters will increase, and smart cities will be in the planning process. There are already commercial appliances like the Nest thermostat that use machine learning algorithms to optimize your energy usage. The Nest is controllable via smartphone app or the Internet, and it provides an element of gamification. This trend will grow and grow, and I am excited to let computers help me make efficient choices in areas of energy, water, and time conservation.

SOFTWARE DEVELOPMENT IN THE FUTURE

Software will continue to be developed in two parallel tracks. One track is software created by commercial vendors that will offer routine updates, technical support, and quality control assurance. The other track is the open source community where work is done mostly by volunteers and a few paid staff. These two tracks will continue, but increasingly the commercial software will need to improve integration with open source software. I remember when the Linux operating system was rising in popularity, and there were those who predicted that Microsoft would be extinct in a few years. There was also the camp that felt that Linux was a hobbyist project and no long-term value would ever come of it. Looking back now, everyone can see that neither group was right or wrong. Today Microsoft still holds a 90% market share over the desktop market and Linux controls 25% of the server market. Clearly neither group is going away. Application software will face the same challenges. Users want a more responsive software experience that gives them easy access (no complicated installs), high availability to needed computing power, and is easy to maintain. The familiarity with instant Web search, wireless connectivity, and the adaptation to the online life has made us all impatient. Software makers will need to respond by ensuring that software enables our style of work rather than frustrating it. Several years ago when I became heavily involved in distributed computing at SAS, I was amazed at how quickly I became accustomed to quick response times. I was working on a modeling problem for a large U.S. bank, and the software was taking about five hours to build a model. When I ported the modeling activity to a distributed computing environment, the model fitting took about three minutes. At first, I was in awe and got giddy each time the models fit in the three- to four-minute range. After a few days, however, if the model took three minutes forty five seconds to complete, I became anxious and started to wonder what was wrong with the system or what other person had consumed the resources that I felt possessive of. This has happened to an entire generation of users. An organization that fails to build performance into its product will become extinct.

Open source projects, especially those supported by the Apache Foundation, will become the standard for software. Commercial vendors in the business-to-business market will continue to exist and thrive because organizations need the regular updates, reliability, risk mitigation, and support that commercial software organizations offer. You will continue to purchase software from vendors just as you do today, but the nature of how those organizations develop software will change to incorporate more open source software. I am not suggesting that all vendors will be like Red Hat, which distributes and extends the open source operating system Linux, but instead open source tools will be the standard within these organizations. The consolidation to certain standards benefits the employees because their skills are transferable from one company to another. Employers benefit because a strong talent pool exists with the needed skills. In this market consolidation, open source will be king. The price, access, and ability to improve are all attractive qualities that ensure that open source software will dominate the software markets to a much larger degree than it currently does. Open source software will be used routinely in more aspects of business operations than it is today, but commercial vendors will still provide products and generate revenues because of their ability to optimize the software and establish more control over the user experience, which leads to a more effortless user experience and higher customer productivity.

FUTURE DEVELOPMENT OF ALGORITHMS

The science of modeling will march forward at an even faster rate than it has already. New algorithms will be developed that in special situations will perform better than stable algorithms that have been around for many years. With the exception of the occasional breakthrough, big data practitioners will need to be well versed in the traditional methods and be capable of evaluating new challengers in objective ways. One thing is certain: The number of algorithms claiming huge advances will increase much faster than the ones that actually move the industry forward. If you refer back to Chapter 5, most of those ideas are really quite old. The newest algorithm inventions will build from these great ideas and show incremental improvement for the next five to ten years. At that time there will be a revolutionary idea that will make a huge step forward in the area of prediction. My personal research interest is in the ensemble tree and deep learning areas. The tools to prototype and express advanced techniques will also continue to improve. DARPA, in early 2013, announced that it would be promoting a new programming paradigm for managing uncertain information. This paradigm will be called Probabilistic Programing for Advanced Machine Learning (PPAML).

As the science of predictive algorithms continues to advance, better predictions will be available. Machines will become better and better at finding patterns in data and skilled software engineers will find more efficient ways to implement these algorithms, the need for human interpretation and oversight will not go away. In the labor-intensive industry of automobile assembly where robots are used heavily in the process. It is humans who have to maintain the equipment and inspect it for faults. No matter how advanced, the computer will not be able to replace the human mind for problem solving and imagination. Computers are not capable of thought; they are capable of information recall. Let us consider Watson, the question-and-answer computer built by IBM, that defeated the best of the best in *Jeopardy!*. Watson is a modern marvel and combines the ideas of big data and predictive analytics as well as any machine I am aware of. Watson was named after the IBM founder, Thomas J. Watson. The system is a cluster of ninety IBM Power 750 servers with a total of 2,880 processor cores and memory storage up to 16 terabytes of RAM. In addition to its impressive size, it is also fast. It can process 500 gigabytes of information or the equivalent of 1 million books per second. With 80 teraflops,[2] it would place in the top 100 of supercomputers in the world. Watson needed so much memory

---

[2] A teraflop is 10^{12} floating operations per second. Flop is a measure of computing speed.

because in order to match human information retrieval times for *Jeopardy!*, hard disk drives would be too slow. Watson uses a number of algorithms to deduce meaning from the questions posed to it in a natural language format. This is a huge step forward for computers that can understand nuance and context. Watson is loaded with dictionaries, novels, taxonomies, ontologies, newspapers, magazines, blogs, and so on—pretty much any electronic media that can be loaded.

As part of an in-depth feature from *The New York Times* in advance of Watson playing on *Jeopardy!*, the computer's processing was described as follows:

> The great shift in artificial intelligence began in the last 10 years, when computer scientists began using statistics to analyze huge piles of documents, like books and news stories. They wrote algorithms that could take any subject and automatically learn what types of words are, statistically speaking, most (and least) associated with it. Using this method, you could put hundreds of articles and books and movie reviews discussing Sherlock Holmes into the computer, and it would calculate that the words "deerstalker hat" and "Professor Moriarty" and "opium" are frequently correlated with one another, but not with, say, the Super Bowl. So at that point you could present the computer with a question that didn't mention Sherlock Holmes by name, but if the machine detected certain associated words, it could conclude that Holmes was the probable subject—and it could also identify hundreds of other concepts and words that weren't present but that were likely to be related to Holmes, like "Baker Street" and "chemistry."

> In theory, this sort of statistical computation has been possible for decades, but it was impractical. Computers weren't fast enough, memory wasn't expansive enough and in any case there was no easy way to put millions of documents into a computer. All that changed in the early '00s. Computer power became drastically cheaper, and the amount of online text exploded as millions of people wrote blogs and wikis about anything and everything; news organizations and academic journals also began putting all their works in digital format. What's more, question-answering experts spent the previous couple

of decades creating several linguistic tools that helped computers puzzle through language—like rhyming dictionaries, bulky synonym finders and "classifiers" that recognized the parts of speech.[1]

The development of algorithms will continue as more success is found in data mining and leveraging analytics within organizations. The law of diminishing returns will apply to all but a select few breakthroughs in the next ten years. This means that most developments will be only slightly better than existing methods.

IN CONCLUSION

The term "big data" may become so overused that it loses its meaning, but the evolution of hardware, software and data mining techniques and the demand for working on large, complex analytical problems is here to stay.

About the Author

Jared Dean (Cary, NC) is a Director of Research and Development at SAS Institute. He is responsible for the development of SAS's worldwide data mining solutions. This includes customer engagements, new feature development, technical support, sales support, and product integration. Prior to joining SAS, Dean worked as a Mathematical Statistician for the U.S. Census Bureau. He holds an MS degree in computational statistics from George Mason University.

When not working, he spends time with his wife and four children. Their favorite family activities include travel, sports, enjoying good food, cheering for the Broncos, and playing games at home.

The author can be reached via these means:

jared.dean@gmail.com

@jaredldean

Appendix

NIKE+ FUELBAND SCRIPT TO RETRIEVE INFORMATION

```groovy
import groovyx.net.http.ContentType
import groovyx.net.http.RESTClient

def accessToken = '17269d534424f87dbfc99c6ac1ab6f4'
def nikePlusClient = new RESTClient('https://api.nike.com/me/
sport/')

def activities = []

def fetchAgain = true
def offset = 1
def count = 10
while (fetchAgain) {
// grab the top-level activities list
 println "Fetching top-level activities for offset: ${offset},
count: ${count}"
 def resp = nikePlusClient.get(
path:'activities',
contentType : ContentType.JSON,
headers: [
  appid : 'fuelband',
  Accept : 'application/json'
],
query:[
  access_token : accessToken,
  offset : offset,
  count : count
]
)

assert resp.status == 200

resp.data.data.each() {
println "Fetching details for: ${it.activityId}"
def activityResp = nikePlusClient.get(
path: "activities/${it.activityId}",
contentType : ContentType.JSON,
headers: [
  appid : 'fuelband',
  Accept : 'application/json'
],
```

```
query: [
 access_token : accessToken
]
)

assert activityResp.status == 200

// add this data for this activity
activities.add([
activityResp.data.activityId,
activityResp.data.startTime,
activityResp.data.activityType,
activityResp.data.metricSummary.fuel,
activityResp.data.metricSummary.distance,
activityResp.data.metricSummary.duration,
activityResp.data.metricSummary.steps
])
}

// determine if we need to fetch another page
if (null != resp.data.paging.next) {
fetchAgain = true
offset += count
} else {
fetchAgain = false
}
}

// write activities to a file
new File("C:\\nike_plus.csv").withWriter { out ->
 // write the header
 out.writeLine("activityId,startTime,activityType,fuel,distance
,duration,steps")

 // write each activity
 activities.each {
 out.writeLine("${it[0]},${it[1]},${it[2]},${it[3]},${it[4]},$
{it[5]},${it[6]}")
 }
}
```

References

INTRODUCTION

The Official Klout Blog. "What does Klout measure?" http://blog.klout.com/2011/12/what-does-klout-measure/

IEEE. "IEEE 802.15™: WIRELESS PERSONAL AREA NETWORKS (PANs)." http://standards.ieee.org/about/get/802/802.15.html

http://www.quora.com/Big-Data/Is-Big-Data-just-a-fad*Big Data: The Next Frontier for Competition*. (May 2011). Retrieved November 13, 2013 from http://www.mckinsey.com/features/big_data.

Davenport, Thomas H., and Jeanne G. Harris. *Competing on Analytics: The New Science of Winning*. Cambridge, MA: Harvard Business School Publishing, 2007.

GNC Staff. "Tracking the Evolution of Big Data, a Timeline.". (2013, May 28). Retrieved June 27, 2013, from http://gcn.com/articles/2013/05/30/gcn30-timeline-big-data.aspx

Hastings, D. "The Challenger Disaster." (2003). Retrieved July 4, 2013, from http://www.core.org.cn/NR/rdonlyres/80850EB6-27D1-4A10-B422-E6383570D5F1/0/challenger.pdf.NationalCancerInstitute.(2013,February8). "What Is Cancer?" Retrieved November 19, 2013 fromhttp://www.cancer.gov/cancertopics/cancerlibrary/what-is-cancer "Tamoxifen." (2013, January 1). Retrieved November 19, 2013 from http://www.macmillan.org.uk/Cancerinformation/Cancertreatment/Treatmenttypes/Hormonaltherapies/Individualhormonaltherapies/Tamoxifen.aspx

Macmillan. "Tamoxifen." (2013, January 1). Retrieved November 19, 2013 from www.macmillan.org.uk/Cancerinformation/Cancertreatment/Treatment-types/Hormonaltherapies/Individualhormonaltherapies/Tamoxifen.aspx

McKinsey & Company. "Big Data: The Next Frontier for Competition." (2011, May). Retrieved November 13, 2013 from www.mckinsey.com/features/big_data

National Cancer Institute. "What Is Cancer?" (2013, February 8). Retrieved November 19, 2013 from www.cancer.gov/cancertopics/cancerlibrary/what-is-cancer

TIOBE Software. Tiobe Index. (2013, September 30). Retrieved October 6, 2013, from http://www.tiobe.com/index.php/content/paperinfo/tpci/index.html

United States Golf Register. (2013) Retrieved June 26, 2013, from http://www.usgolfregister.org/faq.asp.

CHAPTER 2

Dean, Jeffrey, and Sanjay Ghemawat. "MapReduce: Simplified Data Processing on Large Clusters." (2004). OSDI. Communications of the ACM, 50th anniversary issue, 1958–2008 Volume 51 Issue 1, January 2008.

White, Tom. *Hadoop: The Definitive Guide*, 2nd ed. O'Reilly, 2012.

CHAPTER 3

Sony Computer Entertainment Europe Research & Development Division. "Pitfall of Object Oriented Programming." http://harmful.cat-v.org/software/OO_programming/_pdf/Pitfalls_of_Object_Oriented_Programming_GCAP_09.pdf

http://www.statisticbrain.com/average-historic-price-of-ram

Dean , Jeffrey , and Sanjay Ghemawat . "MapReduce: Simplified Data Processing on Large Clusters." (2004, December). OSDI '04: Sixth Symposium on Operating System Design and Implementation, San Francisco, CA. Retrieved research.google.com/archive/mapreduce.html

Eleftheriou, E., R. Haas, J. Jelitto, M. Lantz, and H. Pozidis. (2010, April). IBM Research. Retrieved from http://sites.computer.org/debull/A10dec/ELE_Bulletin_Dec.pdf

Hurwitz, Justin, and Wu-chun Feng. "Initial End-to-End Performance Evaluation of 10-Gigabit Ethernet." (2003, August). Proceedings of IEEE Hot Interconnects: 11th Symposium on High-Performance Interconnects. Retrieved from http://public.lanl.gov/radiant/pubs/10GigE/hoti03.pdf

CHAPTER 4

Kelley, B. (2013, June 26). *What Are the Odds of Making a Hole-In-One?* Retrieved from About.com: http://golf.about.com/od/faqs/f/holeinoneodds.htm.

USGA. (2013). *United States Golf Register*. Retrieved June 26, 2013, from http://www.usgolfregister.org/faq.asp.

SAS Institute Inc. (2013). *SAS® Enterprise Miner™ 13.1: Reference Help*. Cary, NC: SAS Institute Inc.

CHAPTER 5

Bache, K., and M. Lichman. *UCI Machine Learning Repository*. Irvine, CA: University of California, School of Information and Computer Science, 2013. http://archive.ics.uci.edu/ml.

Breiman, Leo, Jerome Friedman, Charles J. Stone, and R. A. Olshen. *Classification and Regression Trees*. New York: Chapman & Hall, 1984.

Cortes, Corinna, and Vladamir Vapnik. "Support-Vector Networks," *Machine Learning* 20 (1995): 273–297.

Ford Motor Company. "Reducing Driver Distractions" (2012, August). Available at http://www.at.ford.com/SiteCollectionImages/2011_NA/Article%20Images/Oct_2011/Driver%20Distractions.pdf.

Hastie, Trevor, Robert Tibshirani, and Jerome Friedman. *The Elements of Statistical Learning: Data Mining, Inference, and Prediction*. New York: Springer-Verlag, 2001.

Hornik, Kur', Maxwell Stinchcombe, and Halber White. "Multilayer Feedforward Networks Are Universal Approximators Neural Networks," *Neural Networks* 2 (1989): 359–366.

Miglautsch, John R. "Thoughts on RFM Scoring," *Journal of Database Marketing* 8 (August 2000): 67-72.

McCulloch, W. S., and W. H. Pitts. "A Logical Calculus of the Ideas Immanent in Nervous Activity," *Bulletin of Mathematical Biophysics* 5 (1943): 115-133.

McGrayne, S. B. *The Theory That Would Not Die: How Bayes' Rule Cracked the Enigma Code, Hunted Down Russian Submarines, and Emerged Triumphant from Two Centuries of Controversy*. New Haven, CT: Yale University Press, 2011.

Nelder, J. A., and R.W.M. Wedderburn. "Generalized Linear Models," *Journal of the Royal Statistical Society A* 135, no. 3 (1972): 370-384.

Neter, J. E. *Applied Linear Statistical Models*. Boston: McGraw-Hill, 1996.

Pearl, J. *Probabilistic Reasoning in Intelligent Systems: Networks of Plausible Inference*, San Francisco: Morgan Kaufmann, 1988.

Pollack, J. B. "No Harm Intended: A Review of the 'Perceptrons,' Expanded Edition." *Journal of Mathematical Psychology* 33, no. 3 (1989): 358–365.

Poole, Michael A., and Patrick N. O'Farrell. "The Assumptions of the Linear Regression Model," *Transactions of the Institute of British Geographers* 52 (1971): 145-158.

Rosenblatt, F. "The Perceptron: A Probabilistic Model for Information Storage and Organization in the Brain," *Psychological Review* 65, no. 6 (1958): 386–408.

Rumelhart, David E., Geoffrey E. Hinton, and Ronald J. Williams. "Learning Representations by Back-Propagating Errors," *Nature* 323 (1986): 533–536.

SAS Institute Inc. *SAS/STAT® 13.1 User's Guide*. Cary, NC: SAS Institute Inc., 2013.

State Farm. *Driving: Through the Eyes of Teens*. (2007.) Available at http://www.cvsa.org/programs/documents/osd/StateFarm_TeenDrivingReport.pdf.

Vapnik, Vladimir Naumovich. *Estimation of Dependences Based on Empirical Data*, 2nd ed. New York: Springer, 2006.

Werner, G., and C. Modlin. *Basic Ratemaking*, 4th ed. Arlington, VA: Casualty Actuarial Society, 2010.

CHAPTER 6

Huang, Minzhang, Hai Zhao, and Bao-Liang Lu. "Pruning Training Samples Using a Supervised Clustering Algorithm," in *Advances in Neural Networks—ISNN 2010*, ed. LiqingZhang, Bao-LiangLu, and JamesKwok. Berlin: Springer-Verlag, 2010.

Zeidat, Nidal, Christoph F. Eick, and Zhenghong Zhao. "Supervised Clustering: Algorithms and Application." (2006, June 28). University of Houston, Technical Report UH-CS-06-10.

CHAPTER 7

Lee, Taiyeong, Ruiwen Zhang, Yongqiao Xiao, and Jared Dean. "Incremental Response Modeling Based on Novelty Detection via One-Class Support Vector Machine" to be presented at the ISBIS 2014 and SLDM Conference in Durham, NC June 2014. Available at http://www.stat.duke.edu/~banks/dcc/.

CHAPTER 8

Al-Naymat, Ghazi. *New Methods for Mining Sequential and Time Series Data*. Saarbrücken, Germany: VDM Verlag Dr. Mueller Aktiengesellschaft & Co. KG, 2010.

Leonard, Michael, Jennifer Sloan, Taiyeong Lee, and Bruce Elsheimer. "An Introduction to Similarity Analysis Using SAS®." SAS Institute Inc., Cary, NC, 2010.

Mitsa, Theophano. *Temporal Data Mining*. Boca Raton, FL: Chapman & Hall/CRC Data Mining and Knowledge Discovery Series, 2010.

CHAPTER 9

"'Next Best Offer' Analytics: Ebay, Schwan Foods, Netflix and Others." http://practicalanalytics.wordpress.com/2012/01/05/analytics-case-study-schwan-foods/

Basu, Chumki, Haym Hirsh, and William Cohen. "Recommendation as Classification: Using Social and Content-Based Information in Recommendation,"

Proceedings of the Fifteenth National Conference on Artificial Intelligence. Palo Alto, CA: AAAI Press, 1998, pp. 714–720.

Bell, Robert M., and Yehuda Koren. "Scalable Collaborative Filtering with Jointly Derived Neighborhood Interpolation Weights," *IEEE International Conference on Data Mining.* (2007). pp. 43–52.

Bell, Robert M., Yehuda Koren, and Chris Volinsky. "The BellKor Solution to the Netflix Grand Prize," Report from the Netflix Prize Winners, 2009. Available at http://www.netflixprize.com/assets/GrandPrize2009_BPC_ BellKor.pdf.

Goldberg, David, David Nichols, Brian M. Oki, and Douglas Terry. "Using Collaborative Filtering to Weave an Information Tapestry," *Communications of the ACM* 35, no. 12 1992, December.

Hinton, Geoffrey E. "Training Products of Experts by Minimizing Contrastive Divergence," *Neural Computation* 14 (2002): 1771–1800.

Konstan, Joseph A., and John Riedl. "Recommended for You," *IEEE Spectrum,* 49, no. 10 (2012).

Koren, Bell and Volinsky, "Matrix Factorization Techniques for Recommender Systems," *IEEE Computer,* 2009.

Salakhutdinov, Ruslan, and Andriy Mnih. "Bayesian Probabilistic Matrix Factorization Using Markov Chain Monte Carlo," *Proceedings of the ICML* 25 (2008): 307.

Salakhutdinov, Ruslan, and Andriy Mnih. "Probabilistic Matrix Factorization," NIPS 2007. Available at http://nips.cc/Conferences/2007/Program/event. php?ID=667.

Salakhutdinov, Ruslan, Andriy Mnih, and Geoffrey Hinton. "Restricted Boltzmann Machines for Collaborative Filtering," *Proceedings of the ICML* (2007): 791–798. Available at http://dl.acm.org/citation.cfm?id=1273596.

CHAPTER 10

J!Archive. http://www.J-Archive.com.

Ken Jennings Detailed Statistics. http://kenjenningsstatistics.blogspot.com.

CHAPTER 17

[1] Thompson, Clive. "What is I.B.M.'s Watson?". *The New York Times Magazine* (2010, June 16). Retrieved from www.nytimes.com/2010/06/20/ magazine/20Computer-t.html? pagewanted=all

Index